Celebs

As for Mr. Leading Man, I was 24 when he first flirted overtly with me over an iced latte. His eyes trailed the dunes of my body and rested on the valley where he relished the sights. All this while, his index finger did a finger-walk on my forearm. I was like, HELLO… I just exchanged friendly banter with your girlfriend and now you're doing the Yellow Pages on my arm while sharing how you bonked my colleague in midair?!

Invisible Panty Line

"What?!" The few of us girls chorused in half shock and disbelief as our eyes instinctively strayed to her body in search for telltale signs of VPL (visible panty line). "Don't you feel naked? Exposed? Cold?"

"Panties are a complete waste of time here. They always end up in my crack anyway." She made a face and pushed her inadequate boobs up. "Ha, but these babies are different. They need all the help they can get!"

Hotel Horrors

The particular floor has its fair share of disgruntled guests who complained of disturbing sightings of what is known as the Japanese Housekeeper… the sudden cold brush of air across the face woke a sleeping stewardess. Her eyes opened to a faint silver-haired silhouette across the room silently bent over her duties. In fear, she shut her eyes tightly and willed the Japanese auntie to go clean another room. It seemed like hours before she opened her eyes again, only to see her seated at the corner of the dimly lit room.

Career Exit Plans

"That girl's so lucky to kena the right combination. Rich man, jealous wife, stupid enough to deliver a slap to her face instead of the husband." My girlfriend Y commented wistfully when I probed her for juicy details. "I want to select my paxs for PR (small talk) very carefully next time."

"Why? Afraid of being the next victim?" I teased.

"No man," she continued. "I want to be slapped! Then I can sue her panties off and quit flying! Ha ha ha!"

Sistas

The girls listened intently, ears pricked as the grand master of erotica, as he so proclaimed himself to be, gave us a lesson on stimulating the senses…

Exasperated, the man pouted his lips in disapproval and asked the group, "Hey, do you girls understand or not?" With his arms held akimbo, he looked around the galley, chanced upon the fruit basket and fished out a Del Monte. "Ok, that was theory. Now for the practical!"

Love is in the air

After the umpteenth passenger, the perfunctory greetings and checking of passes became mundane, to say the least. Then He came along. A lock of eyes and a most beautiful smile was all it took to take my facial muscles to a major stretch, only this time, the reason to smile was personal… My hand instinctively went to tame stray hairs on my French twist while licking my lips to make them glisten. Darn it, why didn't I slap on the gloss before landing?

The Mile Hi! Club

MEMOIRS OF A STEWARDESS

JANET CHEW

PepperConn LLP
www.pepperconn.com

Disclaimer

This book, by and large, is centered on anecdotal accounts of the author's personal experiences; however, the names of individuals, nationalities, airlines, locations, hotels and organisations have been changed.

The book also contains hearsay material retold, and it is not the intent or the view of the author to perpetuate such content as being true, nor to offend or cause malice to any individual or organisation. In the same treatment as the above-mentioned anecdotal accounts, all names have been changed.

The personal relationships of the author described in this book are a figment of her imagination; they are written to be representative of typical relationships of the cabin crew.

It is purely coincidental if any content in this book bears resemblance to any person, living or dead, or any organisation. They are by no means the ultimate representation of any person, airline, hotel and organisation.

Copyright © PepperConn LLP 2009
First print, April 2009   Second print, May 2009   Third print, June 2009
Fourth print, August 2009

National Library Board Singapore Cataloguing in Publication Data
Chew, Janet, 1974 -

The mile hi! club : memoirs of a stewardess / Janet Chew. – Singapore : PepperConn, 2009.
p. cm.

ISBN-13 : 978-981-08-2454-9 (pbk.)

1. Chew, Janet, 1974 - 2. Flight attendants – Singapore – Anecdotes. 3. Airlines – Anecdotes.
I. Title.

HD8039.A432
387.742092 -- dc22   OCN301867614

ISBN : 978-981-08-2454-9

This book is dedicated to the missing piece in my jigsaw puzzle.

CONTENTS

FOREWORD

I was 17 years old when I walked into an interview for a leading airline, in the hope of becoming one of those glamorous girls who flew the friendly skies.

They rejected my application. Apparently, I was "underaged".

So I went back to my fashion modeling career, one I had chanced upon just a few months before this interview. Now I was determined to make the best of modeling, since facing another rejection was not an option for me — at that age. I enjoyed great success in my 10-year modeling career, and subsequently, had a few opportunities to start some wonderful businesses, the most memorable of which was ONE.99Shop.

By then I had forgotten the disappointment of not being accepted by the airline. I never looked back — modeling turned out to be my giant stepping stone — though I must confess that such a life remains a fascinating mystery to me. On many occasions, I have secretly admired those young women who flew around the globe for a living.

Janet Chew's account in The Mile Hi! Club is very enlightening, frightening (for the young), revealing, hilarious, yet truthful. It has a healthy dash of Singapore flavour, yet it is international in every way as Janet offers many vivid stories that take place in cities across the world.

I can't remember the last time I had such a fun time reading about flight attendants and aircrew and the world up there that they live in. This book gives a deep and true insight into the lives of men and women who serve thousands of people every day.

Every job comes with its fair share of expectation management, leadership, problem-solving, politics, fears and rewards. I believe with all my heart that it is not the job that we end up doing, but how we manage the task and goals given to us. Life appears to be full of adventures and opportunities when one has a positive mindset over each circumstance and each season of one's life.

Janet believes, as I do, that at the end of the day, it is hard work that counts. It is what sustains our dreams, takes us to higher ground, and at the same time, pulls us back to earth. Life is about good service to others!

This book is a fabulous personal account and I thank Janet for her generosity in sharing her story.

Nanz Chong-Komo
Best Selling Author of "ONE BUSINESS 99 LESSONS"
Founder Nanzinc.com

PREFACE

"Coffee, tea or me?"

Indeed, the general perception of the cabin crew is limited to this derogatory line. We are often labeled as nothing more than high class waiters or waitresses and in a career that only materialistic, non-academic individuals will pursue. My Dad considered it 'a job for well-paid factory operators.'

My own relatives baulked at the idea. One did not mince her words when she asked why I wanted to be part of the *hiao hiao zhar bors* (narcissistic vain-pots) who buy branded stuff and let leery men stare up their skirts.

Thirteen years have passed. And over that period of time, my old man changed his perception after being fed with countless airline anecdotes and seeing how his sheltered daughter had growth in confidence and character. Despite being in an environment where one could easily be tempted by a myriad of vices and a wild lifestyle, I came away unscathed.

The simple virtues of thrift, integrity and compassion my parents have inculcated are not forgotten. When the door to this exciting domain was held ajar, I went against the odds and kicked it right open.

Thank heavens it did not slam in my face.

I wrote this book for the same purpose of transforming your perception of my often misunderstood and undermined colleagues. And just like how I started my flying career, it started apprehensively.

The first words sparked the first paragraph and soon a chapter formed before my very eyes.

The pun on the word 'Hi' in the book's title is deliberate. As service providers, the smile is not just a PR requirement or merely part of the total service ambience, underneath that smile is a set of gritted teeth - the determination and creative mind to turn a complaint into a compliment.

When the going gets tough, the tough gets going, typically with a scowl and bark; the tougher does it with grace, composure and a smile. It is there in the best and more importantly, worst of circumstances.

I want the world to know that behind every smile, a story awaits to unfold.

I remember a kind, soft-spoken supervisor I flew with, en route to Rome. The man's friendly banter with passengers betrayed nothing of the anguish that ate away at him - a lifetime partner had recently passed away. It was only in the galley where he broke down. Ever the professional, passengers were barred from witnessing the bleeding of his heart. Once out in the cabin, the façade of warm, happy smiles took charge.

As the book came alive with the episodes and eclectic characters that brought meaning to my walk down memory lane, its primary goal is to give due recognition to our unsung service providers. The very ones often taken for granted, even looked down upon.

As for my disapproving relative with the razor-sharp tongue, she has yet to sniff out any trace of the *hiao hiao zhar bor* in her niece. With this mini triumph, I welcome you to the world of the mile hi! cabin crew.

Remember, things aren't always what they seem.

Janet Chew

THE GREENHORN YEARS

1

ONE YEAR TO SEE THE WORLD

Dad made it a point to bring the family out of the country at least twice a year. School hols spelt loads of fun in a foreign place without the worry of unfinished homework and tuition. The latter is enough to dampen the spirits of any school-dreading kid. I was little exception.

I remember sitting alongside my eleven year old brother and looking up in awe at the incredibly beautiful and graceful stewardesses. Angels. That's what they are. "That's what I want to be when I grow up," I whispered into my brother's ear while giving him a slight nudge. I didn't get any response from him. The boy was focused on looking his most mature and practicing his adult voice in preparation for the drink cart service. Don't ask me how, but he managed to weasel a whisky on the rocks out of the sweet stewardess. Not without telling her though that it was meant for the unknowing mum and dad seated a row behind. They did eventually, when he retched after taking a gulp of the honey-colored poison. Until now, he still stays clear of it.

It's no surprise when I left university after a failed attempt to impress the academics; my first job option was that of fulfilling a childhood dream of flying the skies. I scoured the recruitment pages of The Straits Times religiously and my efforts paid off after two months. The signature logo stared back at me from the long-anticipated advertisement. Two smiling uniformed girls sat centre-stage against a backdrop of gulls in mid-flight.

'Lunch in Tokyo and dinner in Paris... with an attractive remuneration of more than $3,500.'

That is a lot of money to a teenager, even more so in those days. The promise of glamour was too enticing. I had to send my application in! The recruitment exercise was on and I wasted little time choosing the best photograph in my possession. Undecided on which to send, I mailed five eventually, hoping to boost my chances against the competition.

It dawned on me that dad would frown upon my decision. The prolific author, who was awarded the Cultural Medallion in 1990, had expected both his children to do him proud in the academic area. Indeed, both my brother and I had done decently enough to be in the elite schools. The day I opted to drop out of NUS's (National University of Singapore) business administration cohort, the disappointed man sat on his favourite wood-paneled bench for what seemed like hours, shoulders slouched like a deflated balloon. It pained me greatly to see my dad like this, but I had used up my lifelines with the lecturers.

Do first, talk later, I decided.

Thousands of hopefuls appeared at the walk-in interview held in a prestigious five-star hotel along Orchard Road. I went confident, armed with prepared answers. Some minutes into the interview, I knew that I was going to breeze through. It turned out to be a casual chat followed by a reading of a passage of which I was able to deliver with ease. Shortly after, I was short-listed and received a letter informing me of a swimming assessment at the training centre.

Being a weak swimmer (read: I can't float for nuts), I take to water as fish to oil. I was apprehensive standing near the edge of the simulation pool clad in nothing next to skinny Spandex. Much to my relief, the non-swimmers were allowed to don a floating device. I later learnt it was at this juncture that applicants were scrutinized from head to toe for visible tattoos, of which the presence of such bodily adornments meant an instant disqualification, no matter how artfully done.

The next selection round entailed a one minute introduction of oneself on stage and a forty-five minute tea party where we mingled with the airline management staff. The applicants were then grouped into fives and given brainteasers to tackle. Natural leaders surfaced as well as herd followers. Some took the opportunity to bark instructions at their team members in order to stand out, while those who hadn't the slightest clue grudgingly took their cue. Then, there were others who guided the laggards patiently without fearing that the latter would slow them down.

What an excellent method of sussing us out in some twenty to thirty minutes.

The following weeks of waiting proved agonizing. Mr. Postman became my favourite visitor and each day, I would race to collect the stack of mail. Finally one with the distinct logo at the corner of the envelope arrived. I literally tore it up in a hurried bid to get to its contents.

The first line, "We are pleased to inform you ..." was enough to set me squealing in delight. After the initial euphoria, I realized the first hurdle had been crossed but now the next was ten times tougher. My old man! He had no idea that his little girl was about to be in the service line some thirty-five thousand feet in the air.

Dad blew his top when I showed him the letter. His blood pressure raised and thick veins protruded visibly from the side of his neck. Mum played accomplice and tried to calm him while playing up the prospects of their daughter carving a flying career.

After much persuasion (and tantrum throwing), the straight-laced man relented.

Not without putting up a fight though. All three weeks of hostility against my silent protests. The stubborn streak of his runs in my blood and he knew it.

"One year," he conceded. "That is all before you go back to your books. One year to see the world."

2

TRAINING DAZE

Training spanned four months in class groups of twenty. Each morning, my dear mum dolled me up and twisted my tresses into a tight headache-inducing bun. Then, twenty minutes would be spent fretting over what to wear.

The dress code was limiting, at least it was for a twenty-one year old girl used to tee-jeans or strappy dress combos. Two-inch heeled court shoes with back-straps ruled in the training centre. Four months! I'll probably have to beg, borrow or steal enough office attire. Not wanting to bust my sorry budget, I spent many a day off scouring the neighbourhood stores for bargain hunts.

The guys apparently faced little problems with their daily wardrobe. "Just five ties are enough," they concurred. "One for each day of the week, coupled with three white shirts max."

That's so true. After a while, I could even tell the day of the week just by looking at their ties. Okay, does that mean that the sole pair of black G2000 pants was going to serve them well for the entire week?

After grabbing a quick bite of banana nut crunch with milk, I rushed out to catch the bus. Missing one meant running one hundred and fifty metres from the bus stop to class. Uphill. In heels.

I was uncomfortable wearing makeup, especially on my lips. It felt as though I had munched through a stick of oily fishballs and forgotten to wipe. Soon enough, I got used to it and the *hum sup* (lecherous) stares from strangers.

These days, I can no longer leave the house without a dab of gloss.

Some of the girls were from Malaysia and in their early twenties. They dressed simply and wore little makeup compared to their Singaporean counterparts. Underneath it all, there were undiscovered gems.

Six years later, one of them was to become the blissful bride to a relative of the royal Brunei family. Another married a wealthy oil executive and moved to New York after a whirlwind romance. Yet another is now the happy wife of an American airline pilot who was besotted with the exotic Asian beauty during their courtship.

Sometimes, I wonder about the lives they are leading now. The clichéd adage of how wealth does not procure happiness may apply to some ill-starred individuals, but in the case of these training mates, at least they've got the bread covered.

I soon became firm friends with a pretty Malay girl of similar height and delicate features. Come break-time, we would chill out under the veranda with a couple of classmates, sharing mild gossips. We complained a lot too. The modules were weighing us down, the diagrams of the aircraft and galley layout baffling.

Frankly, one can picture many possible scenarios but when those in the training videos turn from reel to real, I won't know how I would react.

"Refer to our bible then," offered a senior. Everyone had their version. It was essentially a comprehensive booklet of meticulously compiled notes.

"We are definitely going to *kalang kaboh* (panic) onboard," one lamented.

"No point worrying now. If you do mess up, just smile your sweetest and admit *lor*," another said nonchalantly. That stuck with me. It was to be my guiding motto in the years that followed.

Mess up. Fess up.

Unfortunately, it was under our chill-out zone where I picked up my first stick of cigarette. Call it peer pressure or simply a lack of will power, I didn't refuse the offer when the senior girls puffed away on their Slims and Capris. Expecting the coughing fit that smoking virgins onscreen were seen to break into, I was surprised that other than an initial slight nauseated feeling, I experienced a strange high.

Soon after, I was on a daily diet of Marlboro menthol lights. One before lunch to curb my appetite and another after, while enjoying iced Milo and sliced guava smeared generously with plum powder. Two sticks a day, three max. In order to keep my *fags* (cigarettes) fresh, I hid them in an air-tight Tupperware.

Brother has the nose of a truffle-seeking pig. A bottle of Frebreze sprayed sparingly, took care of that. You never could tell, in case he was to find out and decide to squeal on his sister.

"Why do you smoke?" I remember asking a senior some weeks into my training.

"*Wa liao* (Come on)… it's so cheap. Why not?" He said matter-of-factly. His reasoning might seem shallow but the facts backed him up. At the airport, a carton (ten packs) of duty-free *fags* costs a measly eighteen dollars. That's barely enough for two packs at the local store.

Most stations provide an allowance of at least two packs, thus many smokers would share or split the carton among them. If there happened to be no smoking *kakis* (friends) on that particular flight, the rest of the carton could easily be placed in the 'care' of some junior crew until clearance of customs.

There was a class of twenty guys undergoing promotion training for the rank of senior steward, two of which paid undivided attention to us both.

"So who do you think they're looking at, Isa?" I teased her after the two had turned their glances in our direction for the umpteenth time. It's anyone's guess. While I was porcelain-skinned with shoulder length hair and sharp Eurasian-like features, Isa sported a short crop, golden tan and flawless legs that could go on forever.

"Beautiful girl... wherever you go..." Strains of the song interrupted our conversation one afternoon and we turned around to see the two jokers serenading on bended knees along with their *kakis* belting the backup. As it turned out, Brian, the Eurasian guy had fallen head over heels with Isa while Guo Ren had been trying to catch my eye for the longest time.

Well, he did. How could he not? Apart from the *manga* good looks, the two were singing their lungs out in public and I couldn't figure out which one was tone-deaf and super-pitchy. It was a fawning albeit hilarious gesture.

Double-dating during weekends became the norm. Hard Rock Café was the joint of aircrew and army boys alike. After five long days of sitting our butts stiff and furrowing noses deep into training notes, Saturday was the time for us to literally let our hair down and party the night away.

The only problem was leaving my house in full face paint and party gear without dad's knowledge, which is almost akin to stealing nectar from under the gods' noses. My old man had been screening my phone calls since early secondary school days, filtering unsuspecting suitors who so much as managed a croak when he barked into the receiver.

During the awkward teenage years, I resented the lack of freedom to befriend people of my choice. More so of the opposite gender, of which I was curiously and increasingly drawn to. But not after I met Erica, my neighbour, at the Bedok bus interchange one day after school. The girl was with a guy from the local polytechnic, looking pale and weak. The former had her schoolbag in one hand and a shopping bag in the other.

The transparent plastic bag betrayed the telltale blue and white box of a ClearBlu pregnancy test kit. Later, I learnt that she had gone for an abortion and was thrashed by her father. The man flew into a wild rage upon discovering that the brightest of his three daughters had been naïve enough to get herself knocked up at fifteen.

Alright, no boys for me. Not until I enter junior college anyway.

I took great care to hide those cleavage revealing clubbing outfits well tucked under a trusty denim jacket. Once I got into Guo Ren's flashy set of wheels, out came the cosmetics pouch. The personal decorum training under Lancôme beauticians came in handy indeed. After two weeks of practicing the effects of both warm and cool color spectrum, the makeup virgin in me went from nerdy to savvy.

It was great to be drowned in the deafening rock music and familiar faces. It was an unofficial crew night where we had the privilege of a hefty discount. Jugs of bourbon coke and gin tonic were ordered and imbibed. It was revelry galore.

Not wanting to seem uncool, I downed a few shots of tequila neat and licked the salt off the rim in what I hoped was stylishly done. Its first contact burned my throat and I almost puked. After some fifteen minutes, I attempted a second, then a third followed by a Corona (beer).

Hey, I felt good. I was happy. Before the night was over, I was swooning and becoming Miss Popular. Suddenly, I knew everyone at the club or so I thought because Isa told me the next day that I was all over the joint as if I was Mrs. Hard Rock Cafe.

"I can't find my LV cig holder! I could have sworn I put it into my purse before we danced that night." I winced. My first monogram that had taken two weeks to mull over and a chunk out of my earnings from tuition.

"And was I very high?"

"Half the men at Hard Rock were staring at you the entire night, girl. You were the dancing queen and doing our move so seductively." Isa and I loved to gyrate our hips to the beat. "I could have pounced on you if I were a *L-plate* (lesbian). Think Guo Ren had better tighten the reins on his gorgeous girlfriend."

I laughed it off.

I knew better.

Guo Ren's eyes lit up whenever he saw me. Though he never did once voice his thoughts aloud, it was evident that he was proud of having a natural head-turner as his girl. I was pleased. Others would have paraded their trophy woman if they were in his shoes but no, not him. Instead of showering transient flattery on my appearance, he sought to reach in deeper.

"I discovered the Venus of your heart, baby," he told me once endearingly while gently stroking my shoulder-length hair.

The six year age gap between us proved insignificant as we had much in common. Besides, he looked nowhere near his twenty-seven years. We adored the company of each other and both loved to laugh, at times breaking out in mad guffaws after random ribbing. Being avid lovers of Char Kuay Teow and Fried Hokkien Mee (noodles), we combed the island for the *die-die-must-try* stalls. Quieter moments saw us sharing a leisurely stroll at East Coast in silent companionship. I felt safe in the nest of his strong, tanned arms, knowing that our hearts marched to the beat of the same love-drum.

The first time I witnessed him rescue a hapless mongrel stranded in the massive November downpour, I realized that this attractive man had a compassionate, placid nature to match. He spotted the shivering bags of skin and bones lying pensively on the pavement and before I could go "Look! There's a poor stray out in the..." He was already out in the rain scooping the animal into his arms and loading her into the backseat.

Never mind that we were in our Sunday best and on the way to catch Will Smith's Independence Day. The sweater and mushroom swiss burger intended for the movie came in handy and kept our new friend adequately satiated until we pulled up at his brother's Upper Bukit Timah bungalow.

"Not another one!" Guo Hui held up his hands in mock exasperation. "These pet rescue missions are turning our place into an animal farm." But he too, harboured a soft spot for them and had done his fair share of rescue work.

"Bro, you know how it feels when we manage to find good homes for them. Besides, don't you deny that Bruno and Rags have been a babe magnet for you," cajoled the older of the two brothers.

The two curiously sniffed the behind of the skinny member, tails wagging faster than a car wiper on maximum speed. She looked up at the humans with an expression that said much beyond. Guo Hui let out a soft sigh, stroked the bony frame and wondered aloud.

"Do you think she'll go for Bruno or Rags?" Needless to say, our newly rescued girl was here to stay.

Mondays to Fridays were a drag. The amount of information we had to process in those short months piled up, along with the growing fear of starting our careers in the air. Anecdotal hearsay about crew's untimely encounters with spiritual beings during station layovers compounded our woes. Horror stories about bitchy senior crew and unreasonable passengers didn't help alleviate our anxieties either.

As for me, I took them with a pinch of salt.

Besides, I was really getting sick of canteen food. Save for the sliced guavas.

When training days came to an end, we girls were reluctant to bid our goodbyes. Having ploughed through months of motivational talks, lessons and operations familiarisation together, there was a sense of apprehension as we embarked on the next phase of our journey alone.

On graduation day, we donned our newly tailored uniforms and performed at the auditorium. Many were red-rimmed when the perennial favourite 'That's What Friends Are For' sounded over the PA system.

We knew that among the motley crew, some were going to have the time of their lives while others would throw in the towel after enduring the bond of fifteen months.

As for me, it was my dream come true.

I was raring to fly.

3

SNY Woes

Before we were to become full-fledged flight attendants, the trainees had to undergo SNY (supernumerary) flights on both types of aircraft the crew were trained in. To ease newbies into the job, the company paired us up before the scheduled flight.

On the day of my first flight, my buddy Sherry and I busied with the packing of cabin bags, armed with a list of must-haves and should-brings.

Passport. Check.

Crew ID card and airport pass. Check.

Crew bible. Check.

Crew handbag. Check.

Cosmetic pouch and toiletry kit. Check.

Clothes and shoes. Check.

Undies. Check.

PJs. Check.

Extra uniform. Check.

Bo Zhai pills. (A Chinese herbal medication for tummy aches and the runs. On the insistence of mum.) Check.

Yellow talisman. (Courtesy of aunt). Check.

3. SNY WOES

After a tiring two hours of packing and unpacking, we called each other to fix a meeting point at the airport that night. Reporting time is two hours before departure.

As we strode into the control centre, the rows of cushy seats, vending machines, admin desks and computers greeted us. We checked our flight and the corresponding briefing room number against a huge information board and proceeded to wait quietly outside.

I was feeling uneasy and in the least comfortable. The uniform threatened to squeeze the last breath out of me. It was corset-like at my own doing. The sharp-tongued, bespectacled tailor had warned me when I sucked in my breath in a bid to reduce the digits of my waistline. The full-cupped bra added to my silhouette, not to mention misery as well. That, coupled with the fact that I was wearing full length nude stockings for the first time, made me feel almost mannequin-like.

The eleven rooms in the control centre each housed a TV, chairs, a large mounted whiteboard and a table decked with thick files. Some were occupied and as we peered through the small glass opening to our designated room, we saw a grey uniformed supervisor behind the desk addressing the rest of the seventeen-member crew. His heavily gelled coiffure and outlandish glasses perched on a curiously powdered nose had us whispering to each other.

Is he wearing lip gloss?

As though on telepathy, he looked up and beckoned us in with a wag of his finger.

"Are you two on SNY?" he snarled.

"Yes, sir," I replied meekly. "This is our first flight to… "

He interrupted my line. "Sir? What do you mean sir?! Don't you know my name? Don't you have the courtesy to find out before the flight? Why were you two standing out there like a pair of idiots? The briefing started ten minutes ago and the whole bunch of us had to search for you just now! Didn't your instructor teach you to report straight to the room?!"

"I'm sorry sir… we…" I volunteered an explanation.

"No excuses! If you don't even know how to report for work, you can jolly well go back now! Give me your batch number and instructor's name. I'm going to write you in." (Pen a formal complaint to management)

Sherry remained dumbfounded by the outburst and her eyes started to water.

I could feel the weight of the stares from the other crew members and looked down at my feet. A few threw sympathetic glances our way while others feeling the tension of the situation, chose to look down at their flight notes.

The sides of my cheeks started to flush, drawing heat away from my already cold fingers. The invisible band on my forehead tightened. I now understand the ordeal undergone by the Monkey God in 'Journey to the West'. I wished the carpeted floor could just open up and swallow me whole there and then.

It felt like an agonizing eternity before an angel spoke.

"Relax, Jerome. I'll talk to the girls onboard later. They're probably confused about the proper procedures. We'll punish them by brewing extra frothy cappuccino for you alright? Two spoons of honey." The chief attendant clearly knew how to pander to the man with whom she had several encounters in her eighteen years of flying.

Jerome crossed his legs, *tsk*-ed loudly with a toss of his head before waving us away impatiently.

"Go, go, go… don't waste my time." He dismissed us. Relieved, we took refuge quickly in available seats.

After the safety video, additional pointers were given by the senior ranking crew. Jerome rounded up the session by allocating work positions and ensuring that the worksheet was duly signed. After the briefing, we introduced ourselves to the rest, carefully noting their names in our little notebooks. After the first few, I was lost. No point in asking Sherry, who had yet to recover fully from the jitters. She was just as hazy.

As we weaved our way through the crowded departure hall, approving eyes of the public affirmed our pride. I made a conscious effort to straighten my spine and wear a slight smile.

"It's important to portray a friendly image as long as you're in this uniform, not only onboard," a senior once advised me. "Have you come across a crew member who breaks into a wide smile onboard, the very same snooty one who doesn't give you the time of the day when your paths crossed in the lift?"

Once we stepped into the aircraft, everyone went full steam into action. Ground preparation usually takes approximately 35–45 minutes. First and foremost, the primary crew had to do a thorough check of the aircraft equipment.

Those with a specific assigned even number took charge of heating up foils of moist white face towels and dressing the lavatories with toiletry essentials. Many newbies had faulted in the former, often forgetting to power up the oven after placing the towels in. Others had over-heated the towels to crisp spring rolls.

Another group handled the newspapers trolley setup, magazines, menus and weighty bags of headphones.

The others went about their own set of duties, ranging from starting and testing the audio video system, chilling the beverages and setting the galleys.

There were 101 things to cover in the short span of time but everyone worked systematically. In a flash, the wines and beers were iced, minerals (soft drinks) chilled, meal casseroles checked etc.

Sherry and I stood in the corner of the galley, not knowing what to start with.

"It's natural to feel lost at first. Just observe your mentor and she'll guide you along," the steward told us. "And watch out for Jerome. He'll be pretty active in the Economy Class. Loves to have newbies for snacks," he added with a wink.

How comforting.

As soon as ground preparation was completed, the complex leaders laid out the guidelines and expectations for the flight before a quick touchup of the crew's decorum.

"Crew to boarding stations." Jerome's voice boomed over the PA.

Sherry and I stood at our designated boarding area, chest out, tummy tucked in.

Smile, smile naturally. I muttered under my breath.

It was a Japanese sector, destination Fukuoka, though the profile of that night's passengers consisted of mainly Caucasians. Being a petite 1.58 metres, most of them towered over Sherry. Though she offered to help with the cabin baggage, all declined with a smile with a cheeky one joking about placing her into the compartment as well.

I offered my assistance to a young couple, only to realise that I probably had more difficulty locating the correct seats.

56 AB… 56 AB… where is 56 AB? This looks like 55 and 56… and is A the window or aisle? Think girl, think.

My panic must have been rather apparent because a senior came swiftly to my rescue. She took a quick glance at the boarding passes, smiled warmly and proceeded to bring them to the seats with a tactful "Allow me, Mr. and Mrs. Kato San, this way please. You'll be enjoying the view from the window seat tonight."

"Relax. You had S.O.S. written all over your face. Confidence and professionalism are our best assets. Take the effort to address them by their names and mention the seating position. Many will be appreciative of being acknowledged. This also helps to affirm the seats as some are not aware of what the letters indicate. To the passengers, we are full-fledged cabin attendants. They don't know that you are a trainee and they don't care. A premium is paid for this ticket and premium is what we shall deliver," she later shared with me.

During the meal service, Sherry and I chose to participate. I balanced the meal tray gingerly and prayed that the contents remain intact until it reaches its intended passenger.

So far, so good. Or so I thought, until I poured a glass of red wine for my passenger. Being totally inexperienced, I underestimated the arc of the crimson liquid and could only muster an alarming "Oh shit! I'm so sorry sir!" as his crotch turned an embarrassing shade darker.

The poor man was initially engrossed in his movie and jumped up only when it hit home. I guess my confidence level was not the only thing that shrunk at that moment.

Service recovery was swift. In a flash, Ling, my mentor, removed the tray from the unfortunate victim while apologizing profusely. She promptly came back with a moist towel and soda water but stopped short of cleaning his wet patch.

Clearly embarrassed, the man accepted the towel and tried to wave us off amid the attention it was drawing from his neighbours.

"Give him space." Ling pulled me away. "Read his body language. Don't irritate the passenger further."

The rest of the meal service went on without a hitch. When the meal cart was pulled back into the galley, I realised how tense my whole body was. My neck hurt and mouth, parched. Oh no, did I forget to smile?

Several plastic cups of iced water lined the narrow galley top. "Take five, have a drink," the galley steward offered us. I downed it thankfully. At that moment, never has anything tasted as sweet.

Ten minutes later, Ling checked on the owner of the soiled pair of pants. She returned beaming and gave me a thumbs-up. All that didn't go well ended swell. When the aircraft touched terra firma, Sherry and I were ready to say *Ohaiyo* to the Land of the Rising Sun.

We checked in at the hotel lobby and were greeted by endless bows from the doorman to the concierge to the receptionist. It was not a five-star establishment but the hotel staff exuded a high level of professionalism nonetheless. Much to their delight, the girls were treated to a complimentary pack of coloured cotton hair bands and vanity kit.

Being on SNY, Sherry and I were assigned to share a room while the others had individual rooms. The fatigue of the flight had miraculously worn off and most were chatting excitedly about *makan* (eating) joints and shopping lists. Due to its low frequency, Fukuoka was a flight that was hard to come by for most local crew. It was no surprise that all wanted to make ample use of the overnight stay.

"Sherry! Come, quick!" I yelled from the bathroom.

"The toilet bowl is so cool! There's a series of buttons for the user to press after you are done." I was clearly impressed. I've seen the modest bidet but this gadget before me is really something else.

"There are both warm and cold pulsating water jets with a pressure control and two buttons for cleansing the nether regions, strategically adjusted for both sexes! *Solid* (impressive) right?" I told her after examining the Chinese characters.

Needless to say, both of us took turns giving our royal asses a splash.

When the first jet hit me, I nearly jumped up from the throne. I had underestimated the powerful surge of the iced-cold fountain and fumbled with the buttons in a panicky bid to turn it off. A lift of my body to the side immediately sent a steady stream out between my legs and onto the floor.

I hurriedly mopped up whatever embarrassing evidence of my misadventure with the butt-washer and decided to try the harmless-looking bathtub.

Ah … the bathtub.

Mum seldom allowed brother and I to use that for the simple reason of water wastage. In fact, of all my ten years of using the family tub, I had never actually soaked in it. A big laundry basket holds permanent residence in it along with some scrubs that have outlived their shelf life. Some years back, mum spotted a 15cm long centipede climbing out of the drainage hole. The wretched pest must have found its way up from the pipes connected to the garden downstairs.

Huge mistake. It was swiftly dealt with the first weapon she could get her hands on - the laundry basket.

I ran the water and the tub filled up in mere minutes. Steam formed a layer of mist and before I stepped into the inviting water, I caught sight of my image in the mirror.

Again, I was impressed. The Japanese paid attention pat down to the smallest detail. The body-length mirror was shrouded by a layer of condensation but a rough 20cm by 20cm area remained crystal clear at eye-level.

As I was to discover over the next decade of my flying career, that is a rare feature. More often than not, to rid the hazy layer, it took a lazy wipe against the moistened mirror with the side of a clenched fist. I later learnt a tip from a senior - tilt the tip of the hairdryer at an angle and the mist will clear up in ten seconds.

My first meal in Japan. I closed my eyes and took a deep whiff of the aromatic milky-white pork broth before a sip of the steaming nourishment. The group of six decided on this homely inn some fifteen minutes walk from the hotel, reputed to dish out some serious mouthwatering Gyoza and Ramen.

Appetite satiated, we stepped out onto the streets happy. A cold breeze swept across our faces and my vision blurred. My hand went up to my face instinctively.

"Hey guys, it's raining," I declared as I looked up.

A flurry of cotton descended and Sherry screamed in delight. "It's snow, it's snow!"

I lifted my head and took in the moment with eyes tightly closed. The gentle warmth of the sun. The cool of the falling frost. At that moment, the world stood still.

It was magical.

After some heavy (window) shopping, Sherry and I collapsed onto our beds for a full half hour before dragging ourselves up to pack for the return flight. Our bags did not suffer a hamster binge since little stuff was bought. Everything seemed too expensive. We did, however, get two dozens of fresh cream puffs for a sinful indulgence.

I knew they were a must-buy after Guo Ren brought them to the training centre. The sweet man had persuaded the uncle manning the drinks stall to chill the puffs until I came down for lunch. These creamy delights are heavenly when chilled.

The return leg was chock-a-block (full). Many were elderly Japanese on a trip to Singapore and Bangkok. I was eager to use some newly-learned terms on them.

"Madam, sir… *shiro* or *aka wine deska? Cohi, cocha? Nihon cha?*" I ventured.

The rest of the flight went smoothly until a call light came on. I proceeded to answer the call activated by a pair of aged Japanese. It turned out that the elderly man had earlier needed the bathroom badly but yet waited patiently during the meal service. There was hardly room to contain anything more than a cart along the aisle and he did not want to inconvenience the crew.

Unfortunately, the mind could not control what the body did and he unwittingly wet the seat.

The Japanese are proud people. You can imagine the anguish and anger of both stuck in an awkward situation as such. The crew did their best to make him comfortable with a change of the seat cover and warm hand-towels. Further attempts at service recovery were waved off by the clearly distressed man.

"Be prepared to be called up by the office," Ling warned.

"Some passengers often refuse our gestures onboard, only to shoot a nasty one right to office after the flight. That's worse! Sometimes we *kena* (get implicated) without knowing why!"

An animated Ling proceeded to share her story of how she was called up by the office some two months after a Tokyo-Los Angeles flight. A Chinese lady passenger seated next to a Caucasian mother with an infant and boisterous toddler was approached by Ling in a kind attempt to create more space for the mother. Ling had asked if she mind shifting to another seat two rows back. The young woman obliged with a slight smile, and all was well.

Or so Ling thought.

Months later, she was informed that the irate Chinese passenger had felt obliged to change seats as Ling approached her in front of the mother. The issue of racial discrimination was hurled up. Poor Ling was bewildered by the accusation and shared her side of the story with the administration officer tending to the complaint. Though no penalty (demerit points) was served, the letter remained in her personal file, tainting her otherwise spotless service record.

After the meal, it was toilet checking time. Armed with a toiletry bag (essentially a large plastic carrier bag containing spare combs, toothbrushes, shavers, cream, air freshener and most importantly, disposable gloves), I waited patiently behind the passengers outside the lavatory area. It was peak period and the queue showed no signs of abating.

Ten minutes later, I gave up and went back to the galley.

"Ling, there's just too many passengers waiting to use the toilets," I lamented with a frown. "I didn't manage to clean one at all!"

"What? You actually waited with them? Haha … I can bet that by the time we land in Singapore, you still won't get your turn. You're supposed to explain to the queue that you need to clean the toilets before they use them. Simple as that!"

That was my common sense at bay. Silly me, I thought as I made my way back to the lavatory area again. Once I closed the door behind me and slid the metal latch to the 'locked' position, the white fluorescent light flashed on and my usually insensitive nose caught a whiff of the all too-familiar odour of someone's food, only that it had gone through some intricate bowel distribution. The light brownish remains clung on the inner sides of the toilet bowl in a sorry sight. In a confined area, that was enough to consider a throaty waterfall myself.

The aerosol spray was a godsend. I used it sparingly on the offensive mess, turning my head away while holding my breath and flushed after slamming the lid shut.

Replenish toiletries drawer. Some idiot had dumped a used toothbrush in, smearing the clean ones with foam. Gross.

Spray and wipe mirror. Check.

Pick up trash on floor. Check.

Soak up yellowish puddle on floor. Darn it, I sure hope that's not what I think it is. Check.

Change toilet roll and tissue box. There's still some left. Waste not. Chuck it into the toiletry bag. Check.

Open lid, hold breath and wipe down dried urine stains on toilet seats. Check.

Final spray to suffocate the next lucky passenger. Check.

Some five minutes later, I emerged from the freshly cleaned lavatory, only to be dirtied by the next inconsiderate person who could not bother to dispose used tissues into the bin, nor wipe down the wet sink.

Before the end of the flight, Sherry and I went to the premium class section to look for Jerome, the crew-in-charge. We both dreaded facing him but we needed to get his endorsement on our SNY cards. He was in the galley chatting happily with a strapping Caucasian gentleman with movie-star features. Apparently, the animated gestures and limpy wrist did not seem to put him off as they shared a joke between them and laughed - oblivious to the presence of others around.

Jerome was in a sunny mood. He went through our cards, signed and sent us off with nary a harsh word before turning to his newfound attention-magnet. In later years, I learnt through the gossip vine that he had a penchant for all things blue-eyed and young.

Male, that is.

When the last few tired passengers dragged their feet out of the aircraft, the crew set about checking for any items carelessly left behind. Many years ago, an honest cleaner hit the 'jackpot' of fifty thousand US dollars neatly wrapped in an inconspicuous brown envelope. Really, it is a treasure hunt of sorts. Cameras, cell phones, spectacles, sweaters, wallets and passports are common finds. Needless to say, these all land up at Lost and Found.

The entire set gathered outside the aerobridge while one did a final headcount before they dispersed. Ling handed me a Post-it note with her mobile number on it.

"Feel free to make S.O.S. calls to me okay? My helpline is open

24/7!"

Till today, I am grateful to this mentor who was to become a friend.

The second SNY flight was to Taipei. This time, Sherry and I learnt our lesson and made sure that our supervisor's name stayed imprinted on our minds.

It was the routine scrambling once onboard. This time round, my mentor Suzanne chose to observe my carrying-out of ground duties.

"No point in spoon-feeding you," she said with an air of arrogance. "And please hurry up! I've got my own duties to do!"

With that, she unfolded her arms and held them akimbo. My imaginary head band tightened a notch. I tried to arrange the heavy stacks of magazines on the rack and hastened to free the menu cards tightly bound by yellow plastic.

Ssssss...! I cried out involuntarily. The sharp paper-thin menu cover slid across my index finger and drew blood instantly. The stack dropped from my hands and landed in disarray. Apologizing profusely for my clumsiness, I quickly tried to scoop up the cards.

Suzanne offered no help. The plump girl with a constant frown stared down at me and went, "*Aiyo*, why are you so clumsy? Already so slow and now you go and drop the menus. I've got other things to do okay?!"

With that, she turned and sashayed down the aisle to the galley to fix herself a coke.

Suddenly, I missed Ling.

The rest of the flight proved horrid. I was ordered around by Suzanne whenever the senior steward was absent. She sent me to and fro the galley several times to replenish items that could be done in a sitting, without a hint of appreciation. Instead, her knotted brows indicated that I had taken too much time. How could I not? Everyone was busy with their own duties and I was not at all familiar with the location of the various equipment and food items. I played a version of the variety show game by myself, opening and closing the compartments in the galley in order to get what was required.

I was rapped for lack of speed, questioned for not serving the fairer sex first (the lady had gone to the lavatory) and simply bossed around the entire flight. It was a far cry from the experience I had with Ling and the previous crew working with me. Despite this, I quelled the lump in my throat, swallowed my tears and forced a weak smile.

My third SNY turned out to be a better learning experience.

Mr. Roland Seah, the rotund supervisor who greeted us warmly at the door was a welcoming relief. His popularity was soon apparent as the set of crew relaxed in his presence. Many had flown with him and were glad to see him again. His briefing session was dotted with naughty jokes that would make a prostitute blush. It was totally irrelevant but not a member of the team left the room without a wide grin.

The routine evacuation video was played during ground preparation, followed by a pleasant surprise. Instead of the usual soothing but utterly boring elevator music used during the boarding of passengers, Roland chose to play his own 'Guns & Roses' album. As the loud music rocked throughout the cabin, the crew went about their duties singing loudly. This roly-poly is cool, I thought. The others obviously thought so too and were already making plans for a drinking session with him that night.

I was mentally prepared that it was to be a tiring flight, but the word 'tiring' held little meaning until I experienced it myself. Granted, the passengers were friendly and understanding, but the rate at which they ate and drank was alarming. Some downed each drink faster than one could fix during the drink cart service! My mentor Jessie tactfully offered extra packets of nuts to slow them down and I poured glasses of water for those waiting patiently.

"This is the flight where your knowledge of drink concoctions comes into full use," she said as she placed my 5-by-5 laminated list atop the cart. She was right. I had plenty of orders ranging from simple fruit juices to complicated cocktails. Pretty soon, I was juggling cans of minerals alongside bottles of gin, vodka and scotch. Every now and then, I sneaked a peek at the concoction list.

"Hold the cup by the base, not the top." She reminded me as I picked up the plastic container hastily by the rim. "And place it with the logo facing the passenger. And the ice, try to put it in before the minerals so that you'll not cause the drink to splutter out."

I learnt a lot during the service - the pouring of beer at a slant to create a perfect layer of froth, the method to balance several drinks on the cart top without knocking them down, a gentle twist of the wine bottle to catch the last stray drop, which brand of orange juice needed shaking in order to distribute the pulp and that diet coke had more fizz than regular coke.

We took turns to wolf down the remaining meals languishing in the ovens before prepping up for service two. The girls went around the cabin collecting used items before the distribution of hot towels. The tray of towels was heavier than expected due to the weight of the water absorbed in all fifty wet, steaming towels. I gingerly balanced one on my right arm and held a towel tong with the other.

After a few rows, the weight caused my arm to tremble slightly. I held on and re-angled the tray at ninety degrees closer to my body. Some passengers took forever to acknowledge my offer of the towel while I stood there with a shaking arm and an outstretched tong. The tightness of the uniform cut into my underarms. By the time I made it back to the galley to get another tong for retrieval of used towels, my arm muscles were aching and the right side of my uniform soaked a hue darker, no thanks to the towels.

"You'll get used to it. The drinks are the same, if not heavier," the steward said when he noticed my sorry sight. "There was this stewardess I flew with last year. She was so focused on serving the passengers that she didn't realise that her left boob was leaning onto the Tiger (beer) nearest to her. The froth latched onto her peak some more! Haha... no names mentioned." He slapped his thighs as he recalled the incident.

Well, one thing's for sure. There is a lot more to get used to around here. Grit my teeth. Time to grow up. That pretty much summed up how I survived through my earlier flights.

4

METAMORPHOSIS

Before the company dare set us upon the passengers, clueless trainees are given the lowdown on make-up magic. The transformation is amazing. Small beady eyes open up with a deft application of eye shadow and liner that creates depth; false eyelashes and cosmetic glue completes the illusion. Proper shading on the apple of one's cheeks helps bring out non-existent contours. Red on our lips gives the effect that our pearlies are whiter than they really are. Indeed, the right color combination can make or break a look. To discourage deviant make up experiments, the company conducts frequent random checks on the girls who each carry a color chart depicting her colour scheme.

Guidelines state that painted nails are compulsory and only in shades of red as indicated in one's colour scheme. Painted toe nails are exempted in lieu of stockings; that said, many choose to flaunt fresh pedicures in a matching shade. Raven Red is deemed too dark but the girls love and stick to it anyway. Eye make-up has to be visible from two aircraft doors away, which makes newbies look like *wayang* (Chinese Opera) performers. Gradually, one learns to achieve optimal results with minimal make-up. After all, when it comes to accentuating youthful looks, less is more.

With the mask painted on, it was on to the hair. Back then, instructors were a lot stricter. Many were advised to cut their hair short when they could not manage a neat bun or simply lack the frame for an elegant French twist. Some cried when the chops were delivered. Others vowed to grow their beloved tresses long, the minute they graduate.

When I first started, the tying of a tight neat bun took a bicep-developing half hour. No matter how much I tried to twirl the ponytail into the netting, it seemed to have a life of its own, often peeping out of it. "Your rat tail… no, hamster tail, is too short. That's why it keeps dropping." Isa used to tease me after my hundredth struggle to bunch them up.

Fine. I decided to pay a visit to Fortune Wigs. The lady recommended a neat little china doll style and I liked it. It was a refreshing change to my usual tight, face-lifting bun. It was worth a shot. In the meantime, I could spare my hair some twisting and concentrate on it growing instead.

Dad immediately snapped a picture of my new look. It took centre stage on our family's wall of fame. It felt weird, as though the full head of hair didn't belong to me.

I wonder if balding men with toupees give the game away by subconsciously touching their not-so-crowning glory? I did. Throughout the turnaround flight to Jakarta, my hand instinctively went up to smoothen the already perfect fringe. It was as though to ensure that all whirlwind of activities had not blown my cover away.

On the return leg, a curious passenger asked where I cut my chic bob. She was envious of the jet black, luscious strands. I didn't have the heart to tell her that my coveted tresses came from a factory in Hong Kong. I played along, sharing hair-care tips with the appreciative lady. Well, a little olive oil and avocado butter wouldn't hurt anyone.

My team girl Mary used to highlight the need to observe personal hygiene during tip-sharing sessions in the briefing room. It's true that while the majority of us pay pain-staking attention to keeping an immaculate turnout, the unseen may sometimes be overlooked.

There was a junior girl in my earlier teams, a very sweet petite young lady who ran on Energizer batteries; the enthusiastic girl worked with boundless energy. It made me break out in sweat just looking at her. There was a particular long haul sector to Paris when we both came into close proximity while hanging the mountains of thick winter jackets. I can't recall what she said to me then but I certainly remember the unforgettable and not to mention, unbelievable pong from her pretty orifice.

Mouth that is, in case my words are misconstrued.

Something she had for dinner probably included a dead rat. Out of courtesy, I tried not to cringe. I just ceased breathing altogether for that hour-long minute. Still, a hint must be dropped to the poor girl. For her sake, and more so, the passengers. I grabbed some mint leaves from First Class, squeezed the life out of three lemon wedges into a glass of iced water and invited her to try my concoction. The refreshing drink works like a charm every time, especially when overworked sectors leave me parched and dehydrated.

How do we maintain our svelte figures, many passengers wonder. The larger framed Caucasian ladies love our slender forms. Honestly, if an outsider were to spend a flight alongside our crew, that question could easily be answered. Truly, the physical exertion rivals that of a kick-butt, calorie-busting session at one of the many swanky gyms in town.

Obviously, many of us fall prey to the yummy selection onboard. We tend to snack on leftover fruits, nuts, cheese and mains during lull periods just to stay awake. It is not easy sometimes, staring into space in the still of the night with the symphony of passengers' snores in disconcerted performance. I was a 51 kg size M when I started flying. By the fifth year, I had graduated to an alarming 56kg Size L. My height of 1.71m helped cushioned the weight gain, but I hated the Amazonian frame. In our airline, being a size L is akin to Princess Fiona. The only difference is that the ogre need not cramp her large frame into our wet-suit of a uniform. Each year, I could only suck in my breath when the tailor altered the figures, hoping that she would not notice the ascending trend.

Recently, the airline decided that a re-sizing program was required. Some joked and speculated that passengers had complained that they could no longer glide past a crew along the aisle, with ease. Suddenly, BMI became the buzz word. Crew from all ranks were not spared the compulsory assessment of their indicators, though older ones with a permanent paunch had some leeway, I believe.

Girls who were too curvaceous to fit into even a gunny sack were grounded and sent to the gym for months on end until they could squeeze into their uniforms again. The program proved successful and the passengers could cruise the aisle once again.

5

Look Ma, No Panties!

Our legendary uniform - it is well-tailored to accentuate the female form with such feminine grace that no other could hold a candle to it. The coke bottle silhouette of a stewardess has long been the stuff of many men's dreams. Wet ones included.

The high slit allows active movement in the cabin while the observant can be treated to a hint of leg. When bending down, I took care not to distract the passengers with the unintentional exposure of a coveted flash (flesh) of the valley. The wide collar falls below the collarbone and is tailored in such a way that our modesty is protected. That said, many have cajoled their way into lopping an inch off the standard measurement; tailors have a fixed guideline for necklines. Sure, to some, it is sexy to have one's twin peaks peek out of the uniform while nestled in the snug embrace of the latest *Maximizer*.

But hey, why make it a free for all? Besides, it's what you can't see that tantalizes the mind, isn't it, boys?

I loved my uniform and what it represents. I wore it well and wore it proud. The skin-tight uniform is a double-edged sword. Sensible slim individuals less susceptible to snacking bask in its tailored beauty. I, on the other hand blamed the voracity of my appetite when the zipper failed to lock. In the initial months, it took a bit of getting used to. Its tightness etched marks on the skin resulting in a permanent shade darker. My armpits fell victim to constant rubbing of the fabric whenever I stretched to open or close overhead compartments.

Don't waste your time and money on fade-out creams to rid that. Been there, used that.

During crew rest, I slept in my uniform as I found it a chore to change into PJs. The tightness of it made turning on my side extremely uncomfortable. I could make do with lying on my back for that short 2-3 hours, but the bun sandwiched between my head and the miserably thin pillow protested and strained to stop all blood circulation to my brain. Apparently, I was not alone. A senior girl resolved this by fashioning a curtain with the blanket and unzipping the front of her top. From then on, she slept like a baby in her very own cocooned cot.

She shared this tip with a team girl whose curves tend to suffocate under the uniform. "Why can't we have it in lycra?" she lamented. "Or something elastic so that we can breathe?"

The tip served her well indeed, until one fine day when the blur woman was woken up rudely by the watch alarm, only to find everyone gone from the bunk. She panicked out of fear of being there alone and rushed down the stairs, into the path of a gentleman waiting outside the lavatory. His eyes did a *Roger Rabbit* pop and quickly looked away at imaginary crumbs on the carpet. In that split second, when bosom met cool air, the embarrassed girl hurriedly muttered something inaudible and ran up to the bunk to bury her head.

Lucky guy. It's not every flight that you get an eyeful of mammary 34Cs. Guess he must have spent a longer time than usual in the lavatory.

The stockings proved to be another challenge. Somehow, the carts always managed to play the contact game during service, leaving me with a sudden exposed toe. Having torn numerous cheap one-dollar buys and even resorting to wearing double layers in a bid to cushion the damage, I decided to go with quality. I liked the sense of security stockings gave. Besides the cabin could be rather cold at times and I didn't have the advantage of hair (absolutely zilch) to provide warmth.

A Taiwanese stewardess shared tips on how to preserve their shelf life. Chill a new pair for ten minutes or more before wearing it. Do not attempt to squeeze into a smaller size, thinking that it'd stretch over time; the only thing that would stretch is your credit card bill. Never machine-wash nor peg them. Pegs often cause nicks.

I had my personal favourite available in Australia. We call it 'Qantas' as it depicts two smiley uniformed air crew of the said airline. It is mighty durable and saw me through many years of rough use. The strong elasticity helped stem the network of creeping veins across my legs and provided relief in the form of improved blood circulation.

Stockings take some getting used to. The grip, or rather lack of it, often caused one's sandals to slip out especially during a brisk patrol of the cabin, sending a flying missile across the aisle. Over time, my tightly clenched toes adapted after the initial cramp-up and I no longer bore the embarrassment of startling passengers with a sandal gone amok.

A senior Eurasian girl once divulged her dress code (or lack of). Finding the uniform inhibiting, the spunky lass chose to go without her panties.

"What?!" The few of us girls chorused in half shock and disbelief as our eyes instinctively strayed to her body in search for telltale signs of VPL (visible panty line). "Don't you feel naked? Exposed? Cold?"

"Panties are a complete waste of time here. They always end up in my crack anyway." She made a face and pushed her inadequate boobs up. "Ha, but these babies are different. They need all the help they can get!"

It is a joke amid the crew. The level of *siongness* (hectic activity) of the flight pretty much determines the final state of one's undergarment. Battle-worthy sectors often leave us with literally a G-string. All that squatting up and down rewards us the perkiest of rears without a need to go to the gym.

That said, I'll keep my panties on. Thank you very much.

6

Doctor, I Need An M.C. Please!!

As months flew by, I started to get the hang of things. I began to realise that certain sectors were easier to operate and some stations not worth the trip at all. Soon, I was calling in sick whenever I had Hong Kong turnarounds and other undesirable patterns. More often than not, the sick leave tended to coincide with that of Guo Ren's days off in town. Little surprise there. The person manning the line in the control centre would always be treated to a most genuine sounding cough, followed by a feeble voice reasoning why I could not summon my strength to get out of bed for the flight.

I lived in the East and soon became a regular at the clinic in Terminal Two. The young male doctor was a friendly chap who had patients breezing in and out of his room all day. I often wondered if he could detect that I was perfectly fine even though I was clutching my stomach in pain. I hope that was not too dramatic an act. I figured a woman's stomach cramps would be hard to debate. If he did see through my lousy attempt, the be-spectacled man revealed nothing.

Still, I tried to vary my 'ailment' from time to time. Experienced crew members rub cigarette ash into their eyes to create their own version of conjunctivitis. Very clever indeed, except for the smoking gun - one was questioned by the doctor when she found traces of the grey matter on his eyelids. Migraines topped the list of excuses too. Once, a friend lent me a neck brace to *siam* (avoid) a Manila turnaround. The heavy plastic collar around my neck constricted my head movement. For a while there, it felt as though I was really injured. I looked the part. Confidently, I strode into his consultation room.

The man looked up from the pile of files on his table, took one look at me and went "You are very 夸张 (over-the-top). Can't you find a smaller prop?"

The rush of blush to my face gave me away instantly. From then on, I stuck to stomach cramps.

The unofficial guideline for sick leave is seven days. Exceed that and expect a friendly call from the ward leader. It serves as a subtle reminder that the magic number has been crossed and that the next call would probably not be as friendly.

A team girl from Malaysia hit an astounding sixty days despite repeated reminders from the concerned ward leader. Her list covered petty ailments like headaches, stomach cramps and nausea. Incidentally, those attacks timed themselves nicely when her beau from KL dropped by to visit. We could be considered partners in crime. Our 'crime of passion' is the desperate need to be around the ones we love and loathing the lonely days of being in foreign lands and stone-cold hotel rooms. Only difference is that I exercised more restraint. The moment I hit twenty-five days, alarm bells were set off and I strained hard not to dial the all-too-familiar M.C. (medical certificate) line.

In the fifth year, her long distance relationship finally crumbled under years of pressure. Suddenly, the seemingly sickly girl stopped reporting sick. In fact, earning her keep became top priority. After all, the years of missed flight opportunities did amount to a neat sum. However, it was damage control far too late. A few months later, the contract of five years was not renewed for obvious reasons.

Though the company advises those genuinely sick employees to take due rest instead of running the risk of infecting the others onboard, not all take heed. A chief attendant complained of a nagging pain in the back. He popped two muscle relaxants in a bid to relax those tightly clenched muscles and off he left for the flight. The reason is rather apparent.

With all things held constant, it is a no-brainer as to which candidate management would promote. Besides, the 2003 Sars crisis had clearly shown that those with a flawless disciplinary and medical record held the trump card when the axe falls. The third reason is monetary - stay clean for a year and be rewarded with $350. Meager but hey, it helps with the rent.

I remember my first bout of food poisoning. No thanks to a 24-hour joint near Serangoon Gardens. The next morning, I could barely roll out of bed. I groaned while the deep churning in the pits of my stomach and throbbing on the sides of my head ganged up on me. In fact, I was so sick that it felt as though my time was up.

My folks urged me to call in sick. I was reluctant. Being M.C. free for the last two years, I badly wanted to stick to the squeaky clean record. Staying 'healthy' has its privileges in the workplace. I was in the fourth year of flying and ready for promotion.

I was adamant about dragging my sorry self to work. I figured when it has done its rounds within the complex maze of my unhappy intestines, there should be nothing left to empty. Back in my bed, I popped a double dose of aspirin and *Bo Zhai* pills before curling up to sleep.

That evening, I went onboard feeling weak as hell. The smell of food made me nauseated but I had to stem any urge to shower an unlucky passenger with stomach fluids. Fortunately, I had the better sense to stand by a bottle of lemon and mint water. Taking a few swigs of something citrusy helped, though when I finally saw the doctor in Auckland, I had to have gastric tablets prescribed as well.

During the house call, the friendly doctor declined my offer of coffee and instead, drank readily from the tap. He pronounced it the best-tasting natural water in the world. After he left, I confirmed his belief. It truly was. I realised how delicious tap water is in New Zealand.

I spent the next two days holed up in the hotel room, surviving on the takeaways of bland soupy meals from kind colleagues.

The hell we go through just for that 'clean bill of health'.

There were times when the urge to cough comes on strongly in the midst of service and we had to excuse ourselves abruptly. Leaving the meal cart standing precariously in the middle of the aisle with nice passengers holding it steady. Risk that or cough up zillions of nasty germs. Why go for flight in the first place and take the selfish route of affecting others, you ask? We don't have a choice. Besides, even if we do, the medical leave is a maximum of two days. Have you had a cough or flu that recovers fully in that short a time? I think not.

That said, I promise not to cough nor drip into your drink.

7

A Life On Standby

A typical flight roster consists of both long and short haul flights, as well as standbys. On flights where the crew strength falls short due to medical leave or an aircraft change, the crew on standby could be activated. In the earlier days, crew members were activated for flight duties by an admin officer working from control centre. This was later upgraded to a cold automated voice system that gave no chances, if you fail to answer by the third call, good luck to you. Another crew will be called up while demerit points are registered in your record.

Before mobile phones became ubiquitous, crew members on 24-hour standby had to park themselves dutifully within the confines of their homes.

Our bags had to be pre-packed, one for each category of station we could be called up for : long haul winter, long haul summer, short haul winter, short haul summer and turnaround flights. Now that's a lot of packing to be done!

That is, if any one of us really heeded that advice. Over the years, I've learnt that the good people at control centre would not activate a last minute call-up unless it is absolutely necessary. Or so I would like to think. Then again, a few whispered that even the control staff had a list of favourites, when it comes to high allowance flights like London, New York etc. preferred staff numbers would be called. Way ahead of reporting time, of course.

The conspiracy theory has yet to be proven but one thing's concrete - report sick for undesirable flights and expect to be called for the very same one on the next standby duty. The crew in general second this management decision. After all, it isn't fair for anyone to pick up unwanted scraps. By my second year, I was familiar with the flight numbers and the corresponding stations; even before the entire number was read out, my spirits would soar or dive correspondingly.

Some optimistic crew members liken standbys to a lucky draw of Forrest Gump's chocolates. You never know what you're going to get.

The suspense is enough to ruin the entire day, waiting and jumping out of one's skin each time the phone rang. The worst was the one time when shrill ringing jolted the whole family up at three in the morning. Alas, plans to go downtown had to be shelved. Bleary eyed, I whined and cursed away while throwing stuff into my cabin bag. Poking contact lenses into morning shrunk eyes was no joke. As I made it to the waiting company cab, the observant uncle noted that my nails were nude.

I forgot to paint my nails! As you can imagine, I spent the short fifteen-minute ride not napping, but fighting the bumps and shakes of the cab as I struggled to color the digits. They did not dry on time. I spent the entire flight with curled fingers, hoping that no one would notice the unusual designs on my nails.

When I got more senior and relatively bolder, I took to little sneaks out for movies and the occasional retail therapy. The uncertainty and fear of a sudden call while I was out outweighed the fun hundred times to one. It was in later years when mobile phones allowed the ease of contact that the general lot relaxed. One rule remained for last minute activation : Report straight to control centre within an hour and a half.

Standby duty not only applies when in base but even when outstation. Though, chances of being activated are slim in the sense that no one in his or her right mind would report sick. Reason is simple. Report sick and risk being positioned back (as a passenger) a day earlier, meaning less station and in-flight allowances. When it does happen, the most junior crew member on standby is usually activated, while the rest happily go about their meals and shopping. Chances of the entire set being activated is close to zero, as that happens only when an aircraft diversion occurs. That was what my senior steward assumed.

Few years back in London, he returned to the hotel with his two colleagues after a meal of roast duck in Bayswater. The trio was shocked to see the rest of the uniformed crew members waiting anxiously in the lobby. The good thing about being a steward is the Superman stunt they can pull in times of urgency.

Throw on uniform, dump belongings into bag and hop onto the coach. Ten minutes flat. Just about the same time needed to apply the first layer of concealer on my face.

But of course, the explanation letter took him far longer than that to churn out.

8

LESSONS LEARNT THE HARD WAY

Dad remembers this incident of me calling home from a noisy cubicle in the airport restroom. While changing into my uniform, I realised that the shoe bag containing my all important sandals was missing. Calm and composed I was not, the thought of demerit points during my probation period was too much to bear. The man dragged his napping wife out and got to the airport in record time. Thanks to them, I made it for the flight.

On hindsight, I laugh at how silly I had been. Fancy panicking in the toilet when I could have borrowed from any returning stewardess. Alternatively, a check with the ample stock at Lost and Found - control centre, would have solved my speck of a problem.

I started my first job not without apprehension. The excitement of flying the skies was slightly daunted by the challenges I was to face. The enthusiastic 'I want to join the airline because I enjoy meeting new people' was somewhat inflated.

Yes, I lied through my teeth at the interview. Right through to the mega-watt smile flashed at the panel of interviewers. I was not the typical gung-ho type who could survive in the thickets of the corporate jungle. In fact, I was quite happy to blend in and hopefully disappear into the obscurity and safety net of the masses.

The uniform had an unexplainable way of metamorphosing a public-shy caterpillar to a confident butterfly ready to spread her wings for all to see. I certainly lived most of my flying days as the butterfly.

I was constantly stirring interest among my colleagues and was often singled out. The attention from the boys was indeed flattering. At times, the seniors were curious about my background. Were you a model or beauty queen, they wondered? Others were more intent on malice. I was used to that. Back in school, many girls hated my face - total strangers who did not give me a chance to befriend them, and they, me. I remember walking around the school compound with my head hung low, so that I did not have to bump into any of the arrogant cliques staring daggers at me.

Those who found me a threat resorted to subtle ways to deal with me. Others were more candid. I recall a flight where the senior stewardess and I did not seem to gel. I was patrolling the cabin while the seniors were having their meals. It was my third month of flying. During those days, hierarchy ruled. Seniors ate, juniors checked toilets. Nowadays the leaders should count themselves lucky if there remain a morsel.

When the senior crew finally called me to the galley, I was ravenous. Digging into my lukewarm casserole of stewed chicken, I started to pacify the hunger pangs. Two mouthfuls into the meal, I felt a shadow behind me.

"*Wah*, so slow ah… you think you're fine dining is it? Eat like a Princess," the voice startled me. I quickly dropped my fork.

"Continue la, I also never tell you to stop eating. So scared for what?" the big-boned imposing woman said. She continued to stand next to me, arms tightly folded across her buxomly chest. Expression on her face? Utter disdain.

Now, how in the world was I able to swallow the next mouthful when those watchful eyes of a human hawk were tracing my every move? I attempted a weak stab at the chicken. For the next five minutes, she visually attacked me. Relentlessly. The once delicious piece of breast now lost its appeal. I placed my fork carefully alongside the casserole and stowed away the fowl that had died in vain.

"Why? First you eat so slowly, now you waste food. Not happy is it?" she demanded.

Something came over me. It was time to defend myself. I looked straight into her eyes and asked calmly if she had an issue with me. Simply put in *Ah Lian*'s terms: 'You got problem, is it?'

The startled look on her face showed that the queen was not used to being challenged by the worker bee. She managed a nervous laughter and said something to the effect that she was merely concerned. With that, she muttered an exit and left me alone in the galley, reeling from the near confrontation that could have erupted into a cat-fight.

I may be thinner than her Amazonian-frame, but I sure could deal a mean kick. After all, I did complete the blue belt in *Tae Kwan Do*. Then again, was it worth tearing the seams of my uniform and possibly, stockings too, just to deliver a side kick? Nah.

It has been thirteen years but my relatively short memory still banked in the image of two senior girls who bullied me on a Paris flight. It was a full flight and the multitude of call lights illuminated like Christmas decorations along Orchard road. The set of Economy Class crew were kept on their toes throughout the service, working hard to meet the undulating requests.

Well, most of them anyway. Each time the call indicator went 'ding', they would order me to answer it while they dissected the topic of men. Being the most junior, I obliged, even though my hands were full with ad-hoc requests. I was too meek to refuse. The only opportunity I had to prepare the existing orders was when the senior crew was around. The girls would then do a 180 degree change into eager beavers.

Three quarters into the flight, a complaint came in. Apparently an order of instant noodles twenty minutes ago was forgotten and the angry man (you know what they say about hungry men) demanded to know the reason for the service lapse. The senior steward questioned the three of us.

Bully A feigned ignorance while Bully B hinted at me. Indignant as I was, I kept to my defence with a "No, I did not take this order." All my orders were neatly written down on a post-it pad. I couldn't have messed up here.

The minute the senior steward left the galley, they set upon me. No way was I going to allow myself to be cornered by coercion. I grabbed the silver serving tray and refused contact of any form with both for the remainder of the flight.

Our paths crossed again. Incidentally, some years later, I was the complex leader in the economy class on … what do you know? A Paris flight again! Only this time, the tables have turned. Bully B was still a stewardess due to a dubious medical record.

Did I exact my revenge on her? It would have been sweet.

Well, let's just say that more than a few call lights were answered by our beaver here.

In retrospect, as I reminisce the greenhorn years, I wonder how I ever got through that turbulent phase.

My blunders back then were aplenty. The colleagues who bore the brunt of my mistakes added on to my guilt. The incident that I regret still is my first attempt as a galley stewardess which ended up in destroyed meals - twenty that slipped through my butter-fingers and onto the galley floor with an astounding crash. The scene of the crew rushing around to make up for the shortfall and apologizing to irate passengers remains imprinted in memory. Likewise, when I served meat loaf unwittingly to a vegetarian. My senior was kind enough not to direct the passenger's anger at me when he noted my panic. There were times when my lack of speed caused the rest to juggle more than their fair share of duties. Thankfully, I learnt quickly after each mistake and the blunder index did a nose dive; correspondingly, my self confidence rose.

Someone once told me that a smile gets one out of trifle trouble. A smile from a beautiful woman, on the other hand, saves her from the gallows. Surrounded by my colleagues, I was humbled. Not only were they good-looking, they practically radiated confidence when fielding queries from passengers. I then understood that appearance serves to accentuate professionalism, not overshadow. The common notion that beautiful people have it easy rings true. That said, I meant beautiful from within as well. There's only so long a she-devil could hide her tail behind the cloak of an angel.

To quote Jefferson Davis :

Never be haughty to the humble; never be humble to the haughty.

After scathing encounters with bitchy colleagues, I learnt to stand up to unreasonable demands and outright bullies, with style. I saw no point in stooping to their levels. Seeing how unpleasant some colleagues and passengers could be, I vowed never to replicate their actions. Thankfully, such were few. For the many more kind souls that came my way, I was eager to emulate.

When the going got real shitty, I forced back my tears. Those were the times when I questioned what I had gotten into. On hindsight, what's the point of crying when the milk's spilt? I had only myself to blame and myself to count on. A woman makes herself to fit her clothes. Instead of cursing the skies, focus on climbing out of the shit hole one step at a time.

Some teased me when they discovered that I led a sheltered life prior to flying. I was not geared for the reality of the working world. During the probation period, I struggled to prove my self worth. Alone in the hotel rooms, I bulldozed through the thick manuals, memorising drink concoctions, service procedures and even the entire menu.

Gradually, the check reports were back in the black. For every one brickbat that flew my way, ten bouquets landed on my lap. I was gratified, knowing that it was through plain hard work that had gotten me through.

A senior once liken the airline to a university of society. One grows up fast in the vagaries of this adult world where human nature is at its best and worst. I would like to think that at the end of my stint, I could graduate with flying colors.

COME FLY WITH ME

9

THE GOOD, THE BAD
AND THE UGLY

The Japanese sectors are favoured by most of us. The overnight allowance is considerably higher than that of other Asian stations. It appeals further as its passenger profile fits that of a quiet, non-drinking (moderate) and well-behaved lot. Toilet habits of these passengers in general reflect a high level of hygiene consciousness and civic-mindedness. More often than not, they emerge from the toilet, leaving it in a ready-to-be-used state.

Unfortunately, the opposite could be said about a few other sectors. In fact, stickers depicting flushing instructions in several languages were supplied before such flights so that the crew could stick them appropriately. Not that it helped much. Once, I came face to face with a near overflowing toilet bowl, the offensive yellow liquid within threatening to ebb out at a hint of turbulence. Someone had the lack of courtesy to flush his contribution away while another, the lack of brains to do so before combining his effort!

Some from less developed countries barely knew how to close

the door after them, let alone lock it. As fate would have it, an unsuspecting passenger or stewardess would open the door, giving both parties a rude shock and some spluttering of pee onto the floor.

A steward once struck 'lottery'. A freshly used ("can still smell the iron") sanitary napkin laid smack in the sink. The ends had been folded but somehow, they lost the stickiness and sprung open to greet the disgusted guy.

While bladder juice could easily be whooshed away, human poo posed a challenge. In its solid state, the smell could reasonably be contained when flushed. The problem starts when one has a case of the runs. No amount of flushing is going to rid the brown goo as it clung on to the sides for dear life. There were times when I was tempted to slam the lid shut, empty the spray and certify its readiness, but alas, my conscience always got the better of me.

The trick is to fill a thermos of boiling water from the galley and surprise the shit (literally) out of it to loosen its death grip.

Sometimes, passengers get overzealous with cleaning their private zones and they choke up the towel bowl with tissue, rendering it un-flushable. This is then followed by the next passenger with the runs and thus, creating the worst cleaning nightmare for the unlucky attendant. Imagine the flushing system on strike. No amount of hot waterfall was going to help.

I encountered this several times. Spent every unfortunate occasion revising some four-letter profanity while going down on the revolting pile with a toothbrush. A toothbrush! How pathetic is that? After vigorous stabbing at the soaked tissue, I succeeded in breaking them up into small shreds. In case you were misled into thinking that this happens to all the glamorous stewardesses, no.

No, not because they've not encountered such barbaric toilet behavior, but no, some would rather be caught with their panties down than attempt what I did. The convenient and most commonly sought solution was to toggle with the door status indicator to reflect 'Shut' (in this case, forever as far as she/he was concerned) and then, slap an 'Unserviceable' sticker over the indicator.

Quite easily done, but who suffers the brunt of it when the aircraft touches down? The poor elderly cleaning lady deals with this on a daily basis. So dear readers, the next time you use the loo, take a little time to clean up after yourselves. It speaks volumes about your upbringing and you as a human being.

And while you're at that, you will aim for the bowl, won't you?

Indian passengers love to travel with us, so much so that Indian sectors are always packed. However, these sectors present more of a challenge. The hefty cabin baggage dragged up onboard easily rivals that of cargo baggage. Sure, the size fits most of the time, but certainly not the weight. Some even have the audacity to expect us to heave the one-tonner up into the compartment by ourselves while they stand watching. "What do they have in there? Gold bars?" I jokingly asked a senior in half exasperation.

"Gold bars usually on Dhaka flights *la*, and they buy the seat next to them and guard the bag throughout. These Indian paxs buy lots of heavy electronic items like Hi-Fi and TVs. All paxs are allowed one hand-carry and cabin bag but *dunno* how come always end up with three or four?"

I noticed that too. It is especially rampant out of Indian stations where the authorities apparently acted on their own set of regulations. My girlfriend had the misfortune to assist a passenger with her killer bag; the latter released her hold on the overweight bag just when my friend was ready to push it into the compartment together. The sheer weight of the bag fell back on her outstretched fingers, immediately eliciting a sharp cry of excruciating pain as her finger bent ninety degrees backwards. Another had to quit after her spine was permanently injured in a similar incident.

Baggage related accidents are aplenty. Backaches and slipped discs are common complaints that ring up the cash tills at physiotherapy centres.

The Indians are a discerning lot. Whisky water and of late, whisky soda is the preferred poison. I soon learnt to ask if they wanted ice in their drink, after digging out the cubes from three consecutive orders of coke. The drink cart service is a must because the number of ad-hoc drink orders alone could have us walking all the way to Mumbai and back.

What really got my goat was when one asked for a particular drink and the one next to him would request for the exact drink after I had served the first passenger. With a smile and "Certainly, sir." I proceeded to prepare the second drink in the galley and served him subsequently. This time round, passenger three seated by the window decided that he somehow got extremely thirsty during the two minutes I was away and needed to, guess what?

Order the same drink!

I was like, why didn't you ask me in the first place? Hopefully those thoughts did not reverberate strong enough to be heard aloud. To be fair, this does not apply solely to our Indian passengers, though the high frequency on these sectors had taught me to ask all three passengers for their order. To us, it spelt win-win.

You get good service and we get to save the walkathon.

Being a leader in later years, I absolutely did not condone rudeness. Not from my crew and certainly not passengers at the receiving end of our best efforts. Needless to say that puts the occasional butt-groping, spider-fingering and visual strippers of our uniform at the extreme end of the spectrum. Likewise for the odd few who adamantly tuck aircraft pillows, magazines, service ware, even yanked-out handsets into their bag because they "paid a lot of money for the ticket!" I have done many a Korean flight where elderly folks insist on sleeve tugging and rear smacking to get my attention, despite repeat reminders that there is a call button.

I do not subscribe to the notion that the customers are always right. However, service providers should endeavour to hear them out with an honest attempt to put things right. Many colleagues would take a concerted shot at appeasing an incensed passenger, whom the child in him gave strict instructions to refuse menu choice #2. They would scramble to the premium classes to 'beg' for limited food and *kowtow* (give in) yet again to the *kwai lan* (obnoxious) man before serving the upgraded meal.

I beg to differ. Those with special dietary requirements aside, difficult passengers as such can wait. I don't see why the skeletal crew has to bend over for this single inconsiderate person when the rest of the 300+ nice people are more deserving.

The passenger's level of maturity usually determines my next step of action. Is the sulky passenger threatening never to fly with us again, along with the two imaginary friends in his *Facebook* account? Is he hurling verbal abuse at the hapless crew who could not conjure up his desired meal choice even though "I paid so much for your airline and this is the kind of service I get?!"

Ya right. You probably bought saver seats.

A reader once contributed an article in The Straits Times forum. The rhetorical question touched on the subject of nice guys getting the shorter end of the stick.

Not if I can help it.

That said, our asses have to be covered. A detailed and factual report does just that. It is akin to what cops are made to do by their supervisors when situations go awry. There is a department that handles the flood of reports, each to be dug up when a long-forgotten complaint comes in.

Experience shows that while our Indian passengers are fastidious, they are quick to recognize our sincerity. I found it gratifying to turn a complaint to a compliment. Sadly, that hardly happens with Singaporeans. We seem to come down extra hard on the airline perceived to never falter. Be it a late delivery of The Business Times or The Straits Times (recycled from those who read them first hand), depletion of apple juice or their preferred meal choice, our efforts at service recovery bounces right off their stony end.

During my second year, I inadvertently missed out serving a couple. A service call alerted me to the lapse. With their meals in hand, I offered my apologies profusely. The sullen man with bulging bull-frog eyes took little notice of my regret and berated me audibly in the cabin. There was an immediate cease of activity as pairs of eyes turned our way. The mousy woman tried to hush her partner to no avail.

I stood there trembling in silent rage, swallowing the downright humiliation of being labeled stupid and ordered to get out of his sight. That was the last straw. Thrusting my nametag forward, I invited him to make his feedback known to the office. Wilful? Unprofessional? I didn't think so. At some point in time, we had to stand up for ourselves and salvage whatever pride left.

That drove him ballistic. The man stormed to the galley in search of my senior steward, who bore the rest of his ranting. It was one of those cases when logic and reason slipped off like a novice on ice-skates. The latter gave up and left the man to sulk on an empty stomach for the rest of the flight while I raced to the toilet. The waterworks could not be contained and I cried like never before.

Still, one should not carry her emotional baggage onboard. I dried my tears, powdered the blotchy, sorry sight of a face and psyched myself up with a deep heave of recycled air. Some passengers who played audience to the drama cast sympathetic votes and one kind soul even pat me on the shoulder with an encouraging word. That made my flight a lot less arduous.

Strangely, the call from office never came. Perhaps the report was self-explanatory. Maybe the person-in-charge had read it and clapped heartily in agreement. I don't know, but in a way, I felt vindicated.

Whenever a complaint came, an immediate reaction would likely to be "Singaporean? Oh, no wonder." Racial discrimination issues dominate. The cabin crew is careful not to give any opportunity to be accused of treating Caucasians better than Asians. It is no top secret that the former are generally a lot more affable and forthcoming. The latter hardly toss a side glance at the crew when we sing our 400th 'hello' and 'goodbye'. Most attempts at small talk fail miserably like being in a squash game with a ping pong bat. Yet, time and again, brickbats rain on the ones who chat more with the friendlier and more vocal passengers who so happen to be …Oops! Non-Asian!

I wish they cut our crew some slack.

Passengers from China pose a different ball game. You can hear them from the next galley especially if what seems like half the clan is onboard. The cacophony of shouts and laughter annoys a handful of others but the wide array of Chinese entertainment programs usually work in babysitting the hyperactive bunch. Not unless someone starts on poker cards though. Overall, I found them an easygoing lot. The occasional upsets over not getting their oriental meals of rice or noodles are usually mitigated amicably. Most pack a thermos flask with fragrant tea leaves and are happy to have them topped up with boiling water from the galley dispenser.

Their reference to Chinese tea as 茶水 (tea water) had an impatient crew, who was fed up with the incessant chorus of tea water, throwing the question back at the astonished group.

"你到底要茶还是水??" (So do you want TEA or WATER??)

9. The Good, The Bad And The Ugly

They have come a long way in terms of spending habits. Today, the Chinese share the chummy spot with Koreans on the list of our top in-flight spenders, striking the Japanese and Taiwanese off the charts. These big spenders splurge on timepieces, liquor, cosmetics and basically anything that screams BRANDED. It rarely takes more than mere minutes to decide on multiple purchases, much to the delight of the sales crew who are commission based. Often a sales technique of playing up the popularity and lower duty-free cost seals the deal.

I was promoted to a senior stewardess after four and a half years. The first sales experience on a Seoul bound flight was harrowing to say the least. The minute the sales cart lumbered into the cabin, the Korean ladies practically pounced on the cosmetics drawer. I was caught off-guard and took a few seconds of disbelief before recovering from the shock of countless hands molesting my merchandise.

The initial thought was shit, what if an item or two disappeared amid this mad clamor? Sensing my panic, the seasoned Korean stewardess promptly shooed the prying hands away before shoving the treasured drawer back into the cart. We took down each crazed lady's multiple purchases individually. Most preferred the US dollar to plastic. A full hour later, we staggered back to the galley to stomach our stone-cold meal. That flight alone, I hit a sales volume of $5,400, not bad from the assortment of beauty aids costing more than $100 each.

A friend once received a gift from an adoring gentleman who had slyly asked for her recommendation on a surprise for a sweet young lady. She highlighted the more expensive diamond encased pendant; naturally, as we are encouraged to push the sales up. She was pleasantly surprised when the generous gesture was for her.

Not for long though. Jealous tongues wagged and word got to

the ears of the complex leader, who candidly reminded her of the commandment 'Thou shall not take from passengers'. Indeed, the acceptance of tips and gifts is forbidden though perhaps a small minority is liberal with these gestures. We appreciate these gestures unless the intentions are dubious. A woman's intuition rarely goes off the mark. Such cases warrant a firm decline and a polite 'thank you'. To cushion their awkwardness of rejection, a statement of the trusty commandment would be duly delivered.

Many years ago, I made the acquaintance of Mr. B, a kind gentleman seated in First Class. It was a fully packed and hectic flight to Shanghai, which saw the over-stretched crew of three struggle to juggle their duties. As fate would have it, the butter-fingers syndrome which had long remained dormant decided to rear its ugly head.

Just when I was perfecting a balancing act of eight glasses of Dom Perignon while weathering a slight turbulence. In a haste to serve, I spun around too quickly and the next thing I knew, the Dom was served on the lap of the unsuspecting gentleman enjoying a movie. I guess that was the nearest one could get to a bath in bubbly liquid gold. I screamed in dismay. He yelped in shock. We made a great duo.

Needless to say, I was expecting a tirade of anger directed at my blunder. My crew-in-charge failed to see the lighter side of it and chided me in the cabin. Fortunately, Mr. B recovered from the cold shower and tried to cheer me up. The tall, lanky German slipped me an envelope during disembarkation containing his black iPOD, the very one I had admired, from an earlier conversation.

You might say that it didn't mean much to one who is well-to-do. It might not, monetarily, but it meant a lot as a generous gesture - Mr. B had no reason to console a girl who drenched his pants in fine champagne, much less give away his personal player with initials etched.

10

HOLY SMOKES!

Despite the no-smoking rule, errant passengers still sneak a puff on the sly. Back in the old days, Japanese sectors had a smoking section in the aft cabin. Anyone who has been in a tiny smoking room at the airport would know how it feels to be in one. Even a heavy smoker would liken that to being stuck in an active chimney. The air circulation onboard was already poor to begin with, throw in dozens of smokers and watch the cabin crew attempt a service shrouded in thick smog. As a junior crew then, I was not entitled to choose my desired work position, however, these were the only flights when a junior crew would be allocated the 'choice' aft position as it was a smaller zone. The seniors had better things to do than work with their lungs fighting to draw air.

The first time I patrolled the smoky cabin, I practically gagged. The passengers lit up every other minute, especially the middle-aged and elderly. It stung the eyes and dried out my contact lenses, making service-with-a-smile a lot more difficult to sustain. Everything stank of smoke, from the uniform, hair, right down to the brassieres. Fortunately, it wasn't long before the airline did away with all smoking flights, much to the relief of non-smokers and even social ones like me.

Nicotine-happy passengers didn't like that one bit. The thought of sitting through a long flight without lighting up the happy stick was too much to bear. The company anticipated this and thus prepared the crew for any deviant acts on the sly. True enough, the lengths some would go in order to satisfy a craving. I have caught many emerging from the lavatory pretending that they could not detect a whiff, even when enveloped in a small mist of smoke. Others point an accusing finger at the previous passengers before them. Apparently, the signage stating a fine of two thousand dollars failed to deter. Of course, the culprits deny any wrongdoings when approached.

They literally pull the cover over the smoke detector, using anything from inverted plastic cups to moistened face towels. Most are meticulous, ensuring that the cover is removed only after the smoke has dissipated. The careless few learn the hard way, discovering that the slightest hint of smoke will set off the alarm even after the cigarette is extinguished. I had this particular passenger who refused to open the door despite repeated knocks after the alarm went off. He was probably peeing in his pants by the loud knocking and calls from the steward standing guard outside.

On one occasion, I was alerted to smoke in the lavatories, only to find embers of the stick still bright. Thank heavens for self-extinguishing features of the lavatory smoke detector, or else a fire onboard will have disastrous consequences.

Unknown to public, the crew is slated for an important revision of both land and water evacuation drills annually. SEP (Safety Evacuation Procedures) in airline terms. The nature of the drills alternate, namely land drills and water evacuation in the simulated pool. It is with common jest that colleagues ask one another if they will be wet or dry this year.

Water training frightened me in the initial years. A non-swimmer does not rejoice when the biannual code appears on her roster – imagine standing at the open aircraft door, waiting to be pushed out into the deep pool some distance down below. I was often the last one to jump. As I made the mistake of looking down at the sea of wet faces and tangled hair urging me to follow suit, my legs remained rooted until the trainer helped with a shove.

Surviving a stinging nose from the fall was one. Climbing on to the life raft was another. After all these years of pulling and tugging on the thick nylon rope, I conclude that no girl of human strength is able to heave herself onboard the slippery raft without assistance. The trainers think so too, because an unlucky steward will be appointed to stand at the edge of the bobbing device, ready to pull helpless females up.

Every alternate year, the crew relive childhood days as they leap onto the evacuation slide, clothed in old free-sized overalls and smelly sockettes. Under the watchful eyes of stern trainers, screams and giggles of glee remain muted. I had always marveled at the height of the aircraft, as I slid down the long pumped-up ramp with the proper posture - arms straight, palm facing southwards, back straight and legs slightly apart.

Needless to say, safety training includes fire-fighting. The mockup area is well equipped with galley ovens, cabinets, and extinguishers. The trainers rehearse fire commands and drills before role-play starts. That's where the fun begins. Girls with long hair struggle to stuff their tresses into the smoke hood while the rest hose down a real fire setup with steady squirts of halon. Being inches away from the roaring heat never fails to up the thrill factor. This is also where we have our laugh of the day.

The shout command at the galley mockup is "Inform Captain, galley oven on fire" after a brief act of opening the defective oven before turning to the next person in line. Simple line it seems, but every year, someone is bound to mess up the sequence and spout out,

"Inform Oven, Captain on fire!"

11

High In The Sky

A drink or two on a long weary flight relaxes the body and melts the hours away. For some, the fact that spirits are on the house, motivates that extra can of beer or swig of whisky. Others enjoy a cup of after-dinner cappuccino with some cognac. Whatever the reason, we often remind passengers to hydrate themselves with plenty of fluids. And that, does not include alcohol of any sort.

Whenever we operate sectors with a merry-making profile of passengers, our antennas will fully activate. Experience has taught us not to take things lightly. The crew keeps tabs on the alcoholic drinks consumed by thirsty water buffaloes. This information is disseminated to others in the zone. Frequent patrols are done around party-makers to ensure that all is well. Friendly banters easily reveal signs of their present state. Those who do not hold their drink well or imbibe too many, too fast will start to slur. That's when the serving of more drinks come really slowly. After repeated reminders from the impatient passengers, we would proceed to serve up an in-house concoction of approximately 0.1 percent alcohol and plenty of water.

There are some who simultaneously order from several

stewardesses and down the drinks in a flash. When the effect hits home and the odd few turn rowdy, that's when the real in-flight entertainment begins.

Many years ago, a middle-aged Thai passenger was caught in such a situation. The medium-sized, slim built man with stringy hair started sharing his native tunes loudly with his neighbours. The crew was alerted to the unwelcome songbird and tried to arrest the situation. He turned aggressive and continued the racket at the emergency door. After several futile attempts to calm him down and with the Captain's permission, restraining cuffs were used on him.

I remember standing by with the female supervisor while two stewards pinned the struggling man to the galley wall. In the process, one was bitten on the hand which drew blood. All this while, the cabin service continued so as not to alarm the passengers. With the crew strength down by four, the rest labored to get through the service. Shortly after, the man calmed down and slid onto the galley floor. I was left to keep a watchful eye over him, my heart beating away from the adrenaline rush of the drama that unfolded.

A girlfriend C gave the highlights of her recent Moscow flight. The Russians down alcohol as one would, air. Indeed, these passengers can hold their drink, regardless of age and gender. In fact, we tend to save quite a deal on bottles as many would bring their preferred labels. All we needed to do was to provide ice in plastic cups. On C's flight, it was in ice buckets, on the merry-makers' requests, after the repeated replenishment of the 'miserable ice-cubes' in the cups.

"Their system is seventy percent vodka, confirmed", she jested.

Just the other day, I was having high tea with a few ex-colleagues. One was close to expletives when she related the encounter with an inebriated passenger that left a bad taste in her mouth. The curious group listened on as she related how a Chinese man chose to make an in-flight purchase during preparation for arrival, during which he insisted that his credit card was missing. My girlfriend was very certain that she had returned his card along with the purchase and stated so. The man flew into a rage and started an angry tirade of accusations against her and the entire company who was "out to cheat his money!"

Never tell an angry man to calm down. Likewise, a drunk that he is one. The more the stewardess tried to defuse the situation by offering to check his wallet, the angrier the man got. It was close to landing and she badly wanted to locate the wretched plastic. Without much choice, she advised the man to wait after the plane had landed in order to conduct a cabin search.

When the last passenger had disembarked, my girlfriend approached the man, along with her senior steward. The effects of the alcohol must have worn off a tad, as the man did not protest this time round when they offered to search his wallet. Just in case it happened to be there.

True enough, the card was nestled between the folds of his wallet all this while. Without a word of apology, he mumbled something about the crew wasting his time and lumbered off the plane, leaving the two flabbergasted.

Everyone knows how drinking impairs judgment. Unfortunately, not all take note of that when visiting to the loo, if they make it there at all. Single mindedly on one bursting mission : empty the system. More often than not, experience tells us ladies that even a sober head in the calmest of weather cannot aim for the bull's eye. Thanks to the watering of everything else but the toilet bowl, the crew is left to soak up the mess.

Not all cases of drunken passengers end on a bitter note. I recall an elderly Englishman who sat through half the flight drinking nothing but water. A curious probe and invitation to try the world famous Singapore Sling revealed that he stuck to water, thinking that alcoholic drinks were payable as on many European airlines. After the cheery piece of information that it was in fact, on the house, the old man gaily downed not one, but five of my recommended concoction. Towards the end of the flight, he slept like a baby, smiling and curled up on the stretch of three vacant seats. Just as he disembarked, the nice man pushed a ratty envelope into my palm. Expecting a thank-you note of some sort, I peered in after boarding the cab back home.

What do you know?! One hundred pounds! Those must be the priciest Slings in town, I reckoned. I sure hope I didn't make the endearing man high, but he certainly made me highly happy.

12

MILE HIGH CLUBBERS

Having sex at 35,000 feet in the air does not occur as commonly as one would imagine. Personally, confined spaces are not conducive for such intimate encounters unless you have specially booked the new suites just for that honeymoon experience. That said, the allure of being a member of this club has its stories.

When I did a brief stint as a wannabe at a local TV station, I made the acquaintance of an artiste. He is highly sought after in many leading roles due mainly to his striking good looks and a pair of smothering eyes that turns a toughie into jelly. And oh, that smile of his that stares out of countless prints ads and TV commercials, is one that lingers in the mind long after he has winked goodbye.

He knew he was probably in the top five percentile in the looks and charms department. The girlfriend was on the other end of the spectrum and being an outsider to the industry, she chose to stay out of the limelight. He shared his recent airline conquest, an indecent proposal from a gorgeous stewardess he simply could not refuse. The lure of a stealthy romp in the crew bunk with this sexy nymph blocked out whatever concerns he had. Some thirty minutes later, the Mile High Club welcomed its newest VIP member with open arms.

Or rather, legs.

VIP? Certainly. How many individuals will have the privilege to tango horizontally with a babe onboard? That must have listed top of his little scorebook, one which he proudly shared with me. How they managed this stunt without the notice of others remains a mystery. But one thing is certain, had they been caught in a compromising *Kama Sutra* pose of some sort, our lady vixen here would have to kiss her flying days goodbye.

Many years ago, a stewardess under my charge became extremely friendly with a young and good-looking Australian passenger in Economy Class. It is amazing how chemistry works in a myriad of ways and speed. Before the lunch service, it was more of like "Excuse me sir, would you like the egg frittata or beef noodles?" Some four hours into the flight and an equal amount of PR (small talk) spent, albeit distributed very unevenly, she was practically next to sitting on the lap of her new-found friend.

I remember casting a disapproving look at her when I witnessed the open flirting in the cabin. The audience was watching an unprofessional display by an SPG (Sarong Party Girl – a local term used to refer to girls with a penchant for only Caucasian men) stewardess, carried away by one with blond hair and a razor-sharp nose. She caught my stare, scribbled a note to Blondie and hurried away. During the lull period, I went in search of her when the girl failed to report after what seemed like a long period of time. I was intent on giving her a piece of my mind. Fancy flirting and now skiving!

Having combed the galleys and cabin to no avail, I decided to wait outside the lone occupied lavatory. Some minutes later, I thought I heard shuffling sounds and giggles from within. The unmistakable jingling of a bunch of keys followed. In those days, all flight attendants would carry a bunch of keys. These days, only the seniors do. Intrigued, I decided to tune in for more.

Ten minutes later, the door inched open, as if hesitantly. How strange. Most passengers would simply push the bi-fold wide open. A hand appeared and held the door ajar. Out popped Blondie's ruffled head before he did a 'look left, look right' for oncoming traffic.

Traffic I was not. I was the traffic warden. His startled look betrayed him and he quickly left the scene. I was in no hurry at all. I laid in wait. She emerged shortly, patting her bun in place as she stepped out. Her flushed cheeks would have been drained of their rosy hue, had there not been rouge on her shocked, guilty, 'I-was-just-in-the-toilet-I-didn't-do-anything' face.

As much as it was painful for me, I had no choice but to report her. In my opinion, such unprofessional behaviour can never be condoned.

Back to Mr. Leading Man, I was 24 when he first flirted overtly with me over an iced latte. His eyes trailed the dunes of my body and rested on the valley where he relished the sights. All this while, his hand finger-walked on my forearm. I was like, HELLO… I just exchanged friendly banter with your girlfriend and now you're doing the Yellow Pages on my arm while sharing how you bonked my colleague in midair?!

He was amazingly cute, funny and charming, all rolled into a 1.83m lean frame. But common sense told me that if I allowed things to happen, I would probably end up a statistic. And I do not care to be one in anyone's scorebook, though I wonder which category I would be in.

Model? Stewardess? Maybe there's one under Snow-white and tall, I don't know. How do men categorize their conquests anyway? Appearance, occupation, location of romps or the Wow-factor on a scale of one to ten?

A friend of my brother has his simple Bs, Cs and Ds. 'A' cup holders need not apply.

Another has only one category : anything in a skirt. I suspect he had yet to fill the first page. Skirt chasers are such a turn-off with capital lettered LOSERS embossed on their foreheads.

My last Moscow run a year ago left quite a lasting impression. Not the picturesque sights of the city nor the harrowing winter though. I was patrolling the sleepy cabin after a quick supper service when I chanced upon two individuals who apparently had trouble keeping their eyes closed. The youngsters looked barely out of their teens. The girl, a pretty redhead, was whispering into his ear and giggling when he reached out to tickle her waist.

I smiled at them, finished my rounds and strayed to the business class galley for a little crew chit chat. In crew term, I was zoning - when one from a particular class or zone wanders to another for reasons other than work-related. Typically, members from the gossip vine club itching to work their jaw muscles.

When I next walked towards the sleepless couple, the girl was not at her seat. The boy seemed to be having a bad dream, his brows furrowed and eyes closed. The light from the TV monitor cast a fragmented ray of light on his face, accentuating the premature lines peeking out from the sides of his tightly shut eyes.

Poor boy, so tense, I thought to myself. I sympathise with travelers who have to endure sleepless overnight flights. It is a terrible feeling to be the only few struggling to drift into dreamland when your neighbour is snoring deep in his sleep. All there remain are the ghostly stewardesses floating past your seat with small trays of water, too infrequently and too fast for you to utter 'yes please'.

As I drew closer, something told me that our young man here wasn't exactly focused on getting quality shuteye.

Well, what do you know? Redhead was at her seat, though not exactly sitting on it. Her male friend was clutching what seemed like a ball under the blanket with both hands, the same terse expression on his face. The 'ball' was bobbing up and down. When I told them about the unusual sighting, every busybody did a version of the Bollywood dance, shifting from side to side while trying to catch a glimpse of the action.

13

CLASS

Most wonder how work positions are allocated. Who gets to hobnob with the wealthy and famous in First? Who mingles with the frequent fliers in Business? And who takes care of the masses in Economy?

Supervisors have much leeway in crew deployment. Deciding factors often depend on the passenger load, management style of the crew-in-charge and number of junior staff. We certainly can't have the entire lot of greenhorns holding fort in the same zone.

Some supervisors prefer a balanced mix of senior and junior crew in every zone. Tapping on the best of both worlds – while some senior colleagues lack the spontaneity of their younger brood, their wealth of experience ensures that the latter doesn't screw up. Though, a few will abuse this arrangement by piling more work onto their less experienced colleagues.

Another is a hierarchical approach where the seniors select their preferred work positions, leaving the most junior to salvage the scraps.

Yet another group of leaders prefer to empower the junior crew. These are the rare occasions when those at the bottom get to choose for once. Though it does not necessarily mean a reversal of fortune, as a majority of junior members will still stick to less cushy positions as a form of respect to their mentors. (Or was that just me?) As far as I know, those who happily selected positions normally occupied by the seniors often get bitched about. Freedom of choice? Not in their manual.

The physically demanding position of a galley stewardess is shunned by most girls as it often means breaking a nail or tearing yet another pair of expensive skin-tight stockings. Though, it is favoured by those who prefer not to deal with passengers. However, as it is an important and challenging role, most supervisors will entrust the position to a senior stewardess.

In my early struggling months, working on 747s meant a rotation of the forward economy positions – possibly the worst in the zone. Longer aisles equate to more passengers, babies, frequent travellers and a crew seat facing passengers meant an unavoidable polite conversation at the end of a tiring flight. The lucky ones escape to the aft positions where they could sit right behind and zone out.

Upon my promotion, I started serving in First Class. Contrary to my initial apprehension, I was pleasantly surprised that, in general, the passengers in First Class are a thrill to serve.

Though I wasn't exactly born with a wooden spoon in my mouth, the display of wealth was something I was unaccustomed to. Big French and Italian labels that screamed from the glossy pages of magazines came alive before my very eyes. From the culinary panel of internationally renowned chefs, wine experts to the downy mattresses and duvets for a good night's sleep, every single detail goes into making the cabin ambience a first class experience.

At a single beckon, the stewardess would arm herself with a soft bedding set and clothes hanger. With a push of a few buttons, each seat would be converted to a luxurious bed where the folded corners of the duvet lay invitingly. After tucking the passengers to bed with eyeshades, French and Italian branded PJs and amenity kits, ear plugs and all, we are just a whisker shy of a goodnight kiss. For fear of waking those in slumber, the crew would tiptoe in the dark of the cabin.

Porcelain crockery is stacked into the warming cabinet ensuring that each piece of service ware reaches the passenger's table nicely warmed. What they do not see is the occasional scalding of fingers by the hot crockery. The burn marks on wrists caused by piping racks that produced that delectable slab of succulent tenderloin go unsung as well.

The finest selection of cuisine, wines, cheeses and fruits pampered the elite few, though many do not go beyond three of the courses. In fact, some eat like a bird, preferring to make an entire meal out of caviar and melba toast, which by the way is enough for a return ticket to Kuala Lumpur. Weight-watchers in the form of perfectly coiffed *tai-tais* (wealthy socialites) simply need to point their dainty, manicured finger to the fruit basket. If time permits, we will go the extra mile where the chosen fruit(s) would be washed, peeled and cut into perfect wedges, speared with a decorative maraschino cherry through a swizzle stick.

Drinks would never be allowed to reach the bottom quarter of the glass before an active offer to replenish them. Champagne flutes are chilled before vintage Dom Perignon or Krug is sent bubbling up to the exact three-quarter mark. Once the glass is left untouched for an extended time, it is replaced, bubbly and all.

The spacious lavatories are kept spanking clean and fresh smelling as flight attendants dart in and out each time it is used. Expensive fragrances and lotions line the shelf above the compartment of hankies and orchids. A full length mirror allows a body spin or two. Now if there's an opportunity for a mile high experience, this is the place!

The sight of them boarding with obscenely expensive fur coats and bags screaming for attention was a change from the world I was used to. They take the route of luxury travel as often as I do with the humble bus, down flutes of Krug as I do water and lunch on caviar spread as I do peanut butter. The first time I served this small privileged group, I trembled a little. Not that I was in awe of their deep pockets, but more of the fact that these are treasured customers who pay big money and expect nothing short of the best. Couple that with the uncertainties of premium class service and surprisingly, I did not drop a wine glass or two.

First class passengers in general are friendly, polite and accord us with a level of respect. It is like, hey, they treat us as professional purveyors of the art of service, not mere food and drinks waitresses at their beck and call. Many take the effort to remember my name and thank me for the service rendered. Despite being already accustomed to the finer things in life, they are still without airs.

I remember this kind elderly Australian couple who insisted that I try their main course of succulent marbled beef on a bed of rocket leaves, after I had expressed how appetizing it looked. Naturally, I declined but the gesture left me warm from the heart. There are those who enjoyed talking to me so much that they plonked themselves onto the cold, hard make-shift bench in the galley. There was a kind Indonesian gentleman who encouraged me to return to my books. "Wealth of knowledge is one that doesn't depreciate, my young lady… until dementia sets in!" He winked before breaking out in a hearty laugh.

Then, there were the celebrities. Often with an entourage to fill an auditorium nicely. I had the opportunity to see many in the flesh. A Hong Kong A-list actress looked barely near her 'photo-shopped' image as depicted in her skincare advertisement. The petite lady was pooped. She ate little, slept much and drooled a great deal throughout the flight. Her young assistant mopped her up. Nonetheless, despite being a far cry from her onscreen comic persona, she put on no airs.

Marie Osmond came onboard with her kids and minders in tow and pulled none of the diva-like antics celebrities are known to do. In fact, the beautiful woman, despite fatigue and kids in tow, was all sugar and spice.

Ah Mei, the reigning Taiwanese singer with four-inch platforms practically bound to her feet, was equally obliging when adoring fans among the crew lined up in First Class to get her autograph. Each with a tiny heart-shape dotting the 'i'. The crew went wild.

I shared my thoughts with the other colleagues and they echoed my sentiments. We concluded that indeed those who have 'truly arrived', need not trumpet that fact.

Sadly, a handful of business class passengers earn themselves a bad name. They act as though they have 'arrived' and expect to be treated so, demanding an unfaltering service. And when these demands aren't met, the black sheep among them take it upon themselves to be a big nuisance. They eye the crew with disdain when their stopwatches go beyond the one minute mark for various untimely requests, throw childish tantrums when their meal choices are depleted and often ask for items available from First Class. While the occasional pack of macadamia or a glass of *Cos D'Estournel* is not unreasonable, some abuse the 'kindness' of the cabin crew to ask for more. At times, demand. These are the lot we hate to attend to as it takes a fair amount of patience, pacifying and plain resisting of the urge to throttle their necks.

At times we get requests from business class passengers to invite their friends from economy to join them. This is strongly discouraged as it only serves to disturb the exclusivity and ambience of the cabin. However the chief attendant working there may use his discretion to allow a short visit when the cabin atmosphere is not compromised, usually when the load is light. If it makes you and your friends happy, we might oblige. In short, it is our way of 'give and take'. The problem arises when the visitors find their seats so comfortable that they forget to take their leave completely. After a few tactful reminders from the crew, most would reluctantly down their last drop of sparkly and return to their relatively cramped quarters. However there are times when the 'host' takes offence at the loss of face and insists on them staying since the seats are unoccupied anyway. If only it is as simple as that. Imagine every passenger doing the same. Very soon, the plane would do a nose-dip with the load packed in front.

The introduction of the coffee maker onboard has the thumbs-up from all except the galley crew. A few years ago, the breakfast service offered a standard choice of brewed coffee and tea. The requests for the ad hoc tea like Chamomile and Earl Grey were rare. These days, the order of cappuccinos has hit 'galley high'. Perhaps to the business class passengers, it was simply a case of having a preferred cuppa in the morning, not knowing that each had to be physically prepared by a single steward with 101 duties to juggle with. The frothing of hot milk, brewing of individual coffee-pods, sprinkling the cocoa powder and arranging of saucer is often done concurrently with other tasks. While we have no issues with passengers enjoying their java, it is the lack of patience on their part that irks us. Some expect their drinks and meals to be served immediately, knowing that the crew is already out in full force. The worst are the ones who expect a second or third round of drinks even before the others could be served their first.

Let them wait then, some say; but the complaints would come, others warn. Honestly, you can complain all you want. If the complaints are unjustified, I know that the company would back me up. This airline is not where it is today because it practices the art of *kowtowing* (subservience) regardless of what its detractors might think.

We often refer to them as "not arrived but trying hard to be". The problem is an utter lack of respect for us as professional service providers. Sure, you might be highly paid and you are obviously on a roll and yes, your lush seat separates you from the rest behind. So what? From the crew's stand point, your behavior puts you all the way to the tail end, if not further.

During economic downturns, many business class passengers involuntarily downgrade to economy. While most accept it with certain grace, a few others apparently take a longer time to acclimatize. As I boarded some, the request of a show of their boarding passes was at times, met with a cold stare and the irritated thrust of the slip right in front of my face. A few adamant ones refused to dig into their wallet or pocket yet again, retorting with an indignant response.

"Why do you need my pass again? If I don't have it with me, how the hell did I get through security?!"

These are the times when I really feel like ignoring the fella (sorry guys, but it's usually a man who pulls this stunt) and continue attending to the rest of the peace-loving and compliant group. Can't you understand that screening your pass gives the crew no more pleasure than it does you? But of course, the pain in the 'donkey' could not be disregarded, more so when I was the crew-in-charge of that zone. I smiled all the same and braced for the potential trouble-maker. The stewardess standing opposite swiftly busied herself with the other passengers, leaving the obnoxious oddball in my court. How sly. How it reminded me of early days when I did exactly the same, when passengers intimidated us.

The big man in smart office attire stood his ground while I stood mine. Sorry sir, no boarding pass, no getting past. After a few seconds of standoff, he reached into his breast pocket while I sighed a silent relief. OK, one down, hopefully no more to go. Out flashed a small card. Boarding pass it was not.

"I'm a PREMIUM PASSENGER ok?" The membership card danced in my face before he removed it with a smug look. Here we go again, I thought. Every now and then, we get someone who treats his membership card as though it is a trump card that allows them to get away with murder. I don't get it. Doesn't it make better sense to fish out that elusive pass so everyone could move on? Instead, Mr. VIP chose to interest me with a privilege card that a quarter of the cabin had.

Seeing that I wasn't going to budge, the man finally dropped his bags onto the floor in a huff, brought out the pass grudgingly (which was peeping from his front pocket all the while) and snatched it from my hand after I thanked him.

Thank him for being a childish, uncooperative overgrown brat? No. I was sincerely thankful that he didn't pursue the path of being a potential security threat. Years back, one did and was promptly marched off the aircraft. After the stowaway case to Madras, checks were stepped up by the last line of defence – the crew. Kudos to the company! VVIP or not, toe the line with the security or be dealt with properly.

A local star is basking in the limelight as he is soon to be married. Five years back, the actor was on flight to Shanghai for a movie shoot. The strapping man with rugged good looks came onboard, disregarded my greetings and indicated to his cabin bag with a point of his index finger. I was like, hello… be a man! Surely, it wouldn't hurt to stow your own stuff, much less return a greeting? But of course, as a member of such an acclaimed airline, one has developed a level of tolerance that even Mahatma Gandhi would be proud of. With a smile and a "Certainly, Mr. X", I proceeded to stow his bag, vowing never to watch his serials again. Since the incident, I'm in no hurry to send my congratulatory wishes.

So does this mean that the Economy Class passengers are a lost cause? Certainly not. In fact, it is among such passengers that I have met some of the most wonderful people. Perhaps most of them are in a holiday mood. Maybe they're simply nice folks with no agenda to make other people's lives harder. I've been treated to a snack of home-made Shepherd's pie, given a lesson on tackling Sudoku from a master and enlightened on the joy of knitting. Some suggested a rest when they see me scurry to and fro. Many elderly passengers enriched my flights with a history session when they reminisced. An enthusiastic Indian mother even gave me tips on building a 'nest', seeing how I enjoyed playing with her baby daughter. Others gave that all important nod and smile of acknowledgement, the simple act that adds to the bounce in our step, the curve of our smiles.

One thing's for sure. The passengers we love to love or serve don't belong to a specific class of travel. It is the richness of the mind, the warmness of their hearts that puts them in a class of their own.

And that, is truly first class.

14

WHERE DO WE DRAW THE LINE
ON SERVICE?

We play multiple roles onboard. To some, it merely consists of the primary role of serving food and beverages. They neglect to see the many others we swiftly slip into each time.

One moment, we could be playing porter (undaunted by the guesswork caused by overzealous passengers closing half-filled compartments), friendly usher and lively greeter (repeating the preppy lines countless times and pulling a jaw muscle along the way). The next moment sees us transforming into aviation safety enforcers (sir, this is your last warning. Please switch off the cell or we will all end up in hell), efficient hosts (who race against time to serve up piping hot meals) and the occasional baby-sitters when mummy goes to the *loo*. That is when Junior decides to pine for mummy in an extreme vocal display, drawing the attention of irritated neighbours with accusing glares. If we are lucky to cuddle a peace-loving infant, the latter would be cooed over by stewardess from different galleys. This allows the sleep-deprived parent to catch some shut-eye while knowing that her bundle of joy is in relatively safe hands.

Playing nanny is frowned upon by many supervisors. While the stewardesses' good intentions are apparent, the isolated cases of their charge being returned to the parents in less than mint condition have prompted repeated reminders when it comes to entertaining Junior. Carrying an infant onboard a crowded plane is akin to seeking the treasure chest in a Nintendo game where obstacles are aplenty. Sudden air pockets, stray legs spilling onto the aisle, unlatched galley compartment doors and even the sharp-edged name-tag pinned near the bosom can lay a silent ambush on the unsuspecting minder.

We dabble in the testy role of mediator when passengers' temperaments fray after hours of being strapped in the blood-flow curtailing cramped example of a seat. Many long-limbed ones resort to planting their knees on the seat in front after futile attempts to find comfort without looking like a contortionist. The thin seat backing does not help to pad the alien protrusion for the passenger in front and often sparks off an exchange of words usually not found in bedtime stories. On flights with healthy loads (for the annual report, not our battled selves), getting a seat change is almost impossible. It depends very much on our ability to defuse the situation and seek a solution. Many kind souls have graciously agreed to give up spacious seats (more legroom space at emergency exits and bulkhead areas) to their lanky fellow passengers. Though they ask nothing in return, the crew often show their appreciation via gifts of souvenirs (poker cards, amenity kits etc.) or a guaranteed meal choice.

The medical facilitator in us rises to the occasion when an emergency calls for it. The senior ranked crew are trained in the usage of the AED (automatic emergency defibrillator) to counter sudden cardiac arrest (four minutes is all one has before the brain gives up the fight) while the others play an active backup. There are heroic stories abound. A quick-thinking and selfless stewardess was rocketed to the centre of the airline radar after she sucked the mucus out of the nose of an infant struggling to breathe through his blocked lungs.

Another wasted no time in performing CPR on an unconscious man in a bid to resuscitate him while his colleagues retrieved the first aid and emergency kits. Unfortunately, the force of the chest pumping caused an involuntary regurgitation from the victim's mouth, resulting in a sudden spurt of bodily liquid into the steward's mouth. He later went for several blood tests to lay his worries to rest.

Most of us carry muscle-rubs. This cream, coupled with two Anarex tablets (an analgesic and muscle-relaxant) does wonders to ease muscular aches. The non-stop bending, squatting and stretching, not unlike yoga, rewards the crew with frequent aches and pains. Bruises are the norm. Newbies bear the brunt of arm rests along the narrow aisles and emerged with battered thighs. I would count the little continents of blue-blacks dotting my legs while stifling the occasional outbursts of pain when mum rubbed them hard to "un-clot the blood so that you don't get rheumatism next time." As the months go by, we instinctively learnt to delve smoothly in and out of the seats. Before long, my legs were restored to its original glory.

The muscle-rub cream comes to good use when elderly passengers cramp up after prolonged periods of sitting. Many a times, the crew receives grateful pats on the shoulders while they rub vigorously to set the blood flowing in the feet. Impromptu heating pads devised from hot towels placed in a zip-locked bag provide instant warmth and relief for stomach pains and stiff backs.

An ingenious steward fashioned a thermal bag from disposal surgical gloves, filled with hot water and deftly knotted to form a make-shift hot water bottle. The idea was widely lauded and popularized on night flights where the cabin temperature seems lower.

At times, we receive prior notice of passengers travelling to attend the funerals of loved ones. The tasks of attending to those in grief can be daunting but I had realized the significance of a listening ear, a simple human touch in times of deep anguish. I have had strangers sharing their life stories and breaking down in tears, only to thank me thereafter for the emotional outlet.

Service providers are expected to meet high standards, more so from an airline that many have voted to be the best in the world. How many of us are willing to go far and beyond the call of duty? In airline terms, who would go the extra mile?

Looking at the feet-rubbing, hand-holding crew around me, I dare say there is hope.

A foreign stewardess once remarked matter-of-factly during her third month of employment. "I'm here to serve, not clean the toilets." I was taken aback by the candid statement and more so by the sheer audacity to refuse an instruction given. Who was she kidding? Did she expect the lavatories to be self-disinfecting or perhaps passengers to develop gracious toilet habits overnight? And who in her right mind would counter a senior with a haughty line as such?

"Is that so? I'll check with your ward leader. You must have signed the wrong contract." I said with a tone heavily laced with sarcasm.

She grabbed the toiletry bag and headed for the lavatory in a huff. The cheek.

The others were assigned to other tasks. I saw to it that no one was available to check the lavatories except Miss I-don't–do-toilets.

I might have been a little harsh but she needs to learn the true meaning of service. Sure, no one enjoys cleaning toilets, much less dirty ones, but a commitment to service should take precedence over one's preferences. I was put to that very test myself.

It was on a night flight from Amsterdam, when I answered a service call. When I located the heavyset man with silver-grey eyebrows, I couldn't make out his features clearly until the individual reading light was switched on. I squatted next to his seat and a weathered hand grabbed my wrist. Tiny pearls of perspiration oozed from his facial pores. He indicated an urgent need to use the bathroom located just behind him and I assisted him with the clutches immediately. Less than five minutes later, the handicapped man popped his head out and sheepishly confessed that he had created a mess.

I asked for permission to enter the tight cubicle. Little was I prepared for the sight before me. The putrid stench hit me square in the face but I held my breath, showing no sign of revulsion. He was firmly planted on the toilet seat with his underwear and pants huddled in a sorry pile around the ankles. The whiteness of the former was now smeared with an unfamiliar streak of brown. That was definitely no chocolate sauce.

With a fist clenched tightly on the edge of the sink, he spoke in a bare whisper. "I'm so sorry. I couldn't control at all. This is so embarrassing."

"Not to worry sir… I am here to assist you." I leveled the tone of my voice in order to reassure the distressed man." Let us get you cleaned up first, if you don't mind me. "

Unfortunately, there was no change of fresh clothing in his cabin luggage. I sped to the premium class and with the kind understanding of the crew-in-charge who signed off a sleeper-suit, I returned to the lavatory with an XL-sized pair of grey cotton pants.

He was cleaning soiled areas within reach, albeit with great difficulty due to his handicap. Looking away to conserve both our dignity, I helped him out of his pants and squatted with the opening held wide while he struggled into the new pair. It was tricky to say the least, given the space constraint and avoidance of the offensive articles. Even the shoes were not spared!

"I wish I have a gun, miss," he suddenly spoke languidly, with moistened eyes. "I just want to shoot myself now."

I attempted to lighten the mood by cracking a joke. It fell as flat as a prata kosong and drew no laughter. I continued on a cheery mode and injected life into my voice as I chattered about the flight. Anything to alleviate his anguish.

With hindsight, I wondered how I could have done better in such a situation. I mean, there we were, a mildly suicidal man and lame-joke-cracking girl trying to get out of an extremely shitty situation in a cramped cubicle with the hope of emerging unscathed. After settling the man down at his seat, I went back to the task of assessing the troubled site.

Shoes *kena* (smeared).

Underwear *kena*.

 Pants *kena*.

 Toilet seat cover also *kena*.

Strangely, I failed to understand what prompted me to ignore option 'I-don't-care, I've-done-enough' and to go on my way after a convenient flick of the door indicator to 'lock'. Instead, I went for the 'Are-you-*xiao* (mad) ?!!' option - choosing to wash the dirty linen in private after donning plastic gloves and a liberal spray of air freshener.

A teardrop tickled my vision. Startled, I looked up at the mirror. A reddish nose and tear-strewn cheeks greeted back. Subconsciously, the earlier scene played back while I wrestled with the fumigation and my emotions got the better of me.

Suddenly, I developed a new-found respect for selfless health care volunteers who go through shit (no pun intended) like this on a daily basis.

His head was slumped to the right, a steady stream of snores in sync with his heaving chest. Quietly, I placed the bag containing his cleaned items under the seat and disappeared into the night.

ALL AROUND THE WORLD

15

THE WORLD IS MY SMORGASBORD

The world is your oyster – that is the best part of being a stewardess and the pitch of recruitment advertisements. From food to shopping, you are beseeched with such a diverse array of choices that it's mind-boggling.

But there is an abundance of world gourmet cuisine available on local soil, you say. It's just not the same, I counter.

Believe me, there's nothing like enjoying a glass of Leeuwin Estate Art Series Chardonnay in the lush vineyards of serene Margaret River, biting into a humble but oh-so-delicious bagel along the streets of New York and feeling the crunch of skin as you sink hungry teeth into plump juicy Frankfurters amid the crisp cold air in Copenhagen.

Despite excellent Italian restaurants here, nothing beats homely, honest-to-goodness meals in the cosy setup near the Spanish Steps of Rome where an elderly Italian couple plays host.

Slurp springy ramen in milky seafood broth with noisy locals enjoying sake at a traditional Tokyo inn, oblivious to the bitter cold of winter outside. Enjoy the fresh catch of the sea next to the emerald waters of Fishermen's Wharf where lazy seals sun on boulders. Binge on delectable dim sum with only a sheet of glass between you and the magnificent view of Repulse Bay.

Best mango juice? Definitely a run-down joint in Cairo where the puree-like nectar sweetens the hardest soul amid the hustle and bustle of dusty streets.

Ever tried the local versions of mushrooming Taiwanese and Hong Kong cafes? What's your rating? I know mine comes out tops. Tops in the 'been-there, tried-that, won't-ever-go-back-again' category, that is. Local stalls fail miserably in their attempt to replicate the taste of the ubiquitous, finger-licking fried chicken cutlets found in every Taiwan night market.

What tickles me most is the dish that never fails to appear on the menus of self-proclaimed Singapore restaurants all over the world - Singapore fried noodles. This fried version of vermicelli with a strong hint of curry spices is one that I have never tasted locally in all my years as a true blue Singaporean. Then again, the French didn't invent French fries either. The Belgians claim they did.

Everyone has their favourite stations. Our Muslim counterparts prefer places where halal food is readily available. Many avoid Mandarin-speaking routes where language barriers are an obvious deterrent.

I love Taipei. And usually upon touchdown, no time is wasted. After a hot shower (the tub can wait), we would hurry to the famous 士林 (Shih Lin) night market - which is popular with both locals and tourists alike. Dormant in the day, it comes alive when the sun sets with countless stalls bearing neon signs selling anything and everything - clothes, shoes, kitchenware, herbal medicines, guppies and puppies!

We would stride along the bustling streets after a gastronomic encounter of 臭豆腐 (fermented bean curd) and oyster 面线 (noodles). The notoriously pungent fried bean curd can be detected a mile away. The snaking queue does not daunt its many fans.

Imagine biting into golden cubes filled with velvety white flesh, throw in vinegarish chilli with a sprinkling of sesame seeds that adds a twist to the sinful gush of oil oozing out - I could have sworn it gave me a heady spin when I took my first bite. It was a culinary match in heaven.

The Taiwanese like their meat braised. Many stalls sell trotters and intestinal organs slapped on a small heap of steaming white rice accompanied by pepper-laced pork broth.

Squid has never been my preferred seafood but the Taiwanese version with a lethal combination of special seasoning and chilli, along with the crispy yet tender calamari made me view it in a different light. Generous sprigs of basil are fried to a crisp and mixed in, giving an interesting lilt to the burst of flavours.

Japanese cities have always been top on the list of the crew. Be it Tokyo, Osaka, Hiroshima or Fukuoka, these favourite stations get a resounding 'Hai!' In fact, many scour the 'Change of Flights' notice board online in a futile bid to try to offer their flights for these highly in-demand stations. It is like a market where flights are offered and countered-offered, but with a strict 'No monetary terms' rule. As to how much this rule is flexed behind closed doors, no one knows.

There are food joints in every flight destination with our stamp of approval, literally. Some have become friends over years of steadfast patronage and owners proudly stick the label of our airline logo at the entrance.

It is known that a popular Chinese restaurant in Amsterdam started out nowhere near its present size. The new establishment had no accolades to its name though the quality of its dishes justified otherwise. The humble and affable owner welcomed us and made it a point to throw in a ten percent discount. Little details were noted. Glasses of iced water and vital bowls of chopped red chilli appeared automatically. Generous servings of dessert were on the house.

By word of mouth, the cabin crew started to dine there in big groups. The herd mentality worked in the owner's favour. The crowds poured in and soon, the restaurant swelled in size while retaining its service standards.

The same cannot be said for a certain restaurant famous for its roast duck in London's Bayswater. Their staff treats airline crews with slight disdain. Maybe we are too boisterous. I don't know. The roast duck may be one of the best in London but that certainly did not stop us from migrating to its competitor – The Gold Mine. It certainly gives the former a run for its pounds.

With the delectable duck, equally essential red chilli, complimentary pork rib peanut soup and naval orange wedges, we are at peace once more.

Reminiscing the places and food that I've tasted, loved and hated - I am glad I kicked that door open some thirteen years ago. Without which, I would not have had the pleasure of dining and wining around the world, turning it into my personal smorgasbord.

I'm mighty glad that I did.

16

THE REAL DEAL

To the observant traveler, the standard practice of some airlines is to provide a coordinated set of luggage for the crew. Black is the preferred color, withstanding the test of time and tide.

Not ours though. We beg to differ and bask in a little more originality. Where cargo bags are concerned, Samsonite and Delsey rules. When it comes to cabin totes, seasons change, 'It' bags came and went. Louis Vuitton (LV), the leather darling; however, remains evergreen and unanimous among men and women alike. A glide of fingers across the seamless stitches of each masterpiece is sufficient to break the dams of one's common sense and possibly, the piggy bank.

While it is true the price may seem extravagant to some and cast an unflattering light on its users, fans have their piece of reasoning. Do we even need an excuse in the first place? A girlfriend once joked about how her trusty Damier Speedy had outlasted three regrettable relationships. When tears are spilled, at least Louis thrilled.

Indeed, the quality of a genuine product far surpasses an inferior copy bag. My first tote bought from the Raffles Hotel boutique way back in 1996 is still in perfect condition. Give it a good sniff and the unmistakable leather scent floats right through the nostrils.

During a trip to Seoul in the first year, I tagged along with the seniors to the tourist belt of Itaewon. A multitude of shops were touting fake luxury items from Rolex watches, Gucci shoes, Chanel stockings to LV goods. The enthusiastic shop keepers badgered tourists, second-guessing their nationality and switched to the appropriate language. I was rather impressed with one who danced between splatters of Mandarin, English, Japanese and Thai. If I had his flair for foreign languages, I would face fewer stumbling blocks with my passengers.

Undeterred, the seniors knew exactly where they were headed. After a few small winding paths, we arrived at a shop popular with the crew. In fact, by word-of-mouth, it had become THE shop. The petite lady boss, affectionately known as Wendy, was welcoming. She smiled so widely that her small eye slits merged into the folds of her crowfeet-like wrinkles.

She whispered into the ear of my senior steward and we proceeded to follow the high-spirited lady down yet another few winding paths to her abode, VIP access only. There we sat cross-legged on the parquet floor for the next two hours, all eight of us, scrutinizing the details of each item she piled in front of us.

"AA grade, very good quality, very cheap!" she exclaimed with each price query she entertained. She must have aced her math. The woman breezed through each switching of currency, from Singapore dollars to Korean won to the greenback, with the calculator embedded in her head of curly locks.

The group literally tossed their purchases into shopping baskets. The lists were long, no thanks to friends and relatives back home. I succumbed to a blue leather wallet. The traveler version in my favourite shade felt good in my hands, especially when it cost a fraction of the original. Does it look real? Does it look real? I pestered the seniors.

"Exactly like the real thing, can buy, can buy." The seasoned colleagues assured me as they sussed out the Prada postman bags.

When it comes to group haggling, believe me, the local crew are mighty good at this. It left us all beaming with our new conquests and Wendy with a fat wad of cash in her 'AA' grade Prada waist pouch.

When the wallet died on me a few months later, I blamed no one but myself. The PVC layer and threads gave way to rough handling and constant abrasion whenever I tried to squeeze it into my overstuffed handbag. It became painfully shy to display it in public view and so I decided to give my first *cheong* (fake) possession a rest along with the trash.

Even as I stayed away from the fake stuff, it didn't mean that I blew it all on branded goods. Contrary to the general perception, stewardesses are not all wanton spenders.

As the saying goes - fingers of the same palm but each a different length. So is every stewardess. In the public eye, we lead a glamorous lifestyle - shopping, partying and dining at the trendiest strips around the world. Many of us are walking endorsements for the big brands. While some barely blink when they sign away their last-drawn paycheck on the latest trends, others are contented to spend sensibly.

I know a couple who are both senior attendants with a comfortable combined salary of eleven thousand. The girl is happy in her Giordano togs and Charles & Keith heels while her husband is just as comfortable with food court meals and the occasional home cooked grub. A Malaysian girl from my team scrimps as much as she can and remits at least two thousand monthly back home to Kuala Lumpur. A few invested their earnings in property during the lull. One is now sitting contentedly on the rental yields from two condominiums and a double-story shop house. Not too bad for a guy who left school after completing the O levels, don't you think?

17

ARE WE ALONE?

Outsiders wonder how we do it. Drifting off peacefully into the land of zero-calorie triple chocolate cheesecakes and striking Toto (lottery) every night, cooped within four cold walls of a strange hotel room and where a member from *Monsters Inc* could pounce the minute the lights go off?

My aunt insisted on a yellow talisman from the famous temple in *Si Bei Lo*. She rationalized that the Hades gatekeeper might not be meticulous in his headcount at the end of the Hungry Ghosts Festival. "There are some who managed to give the gatekeepers the slip," she said. I was neither superstitious nor paranoid but who wants to take chances when all it takes to have peace of mind was to tuck the yellow triangular fold into my wallet?

Some girls of a more timid nature will prefer to bunk in with other like-minded colleagues. These are few and far between, simply because most of us guard our privacy like a ferocious dog. Sleeping patterns differ. Bathroom manners do too. I for one can never share a room for the fact that I prefer to let my skin breathe. Can't do that very well with clothes on, can I? In fact, I know a few who can't sleep in anything more than their birthday suits.

The next best solution is to seek the reception lady's help in getting a room allocated as close to other colleagues as possible. Better still if it's connecting rooms with an emergency side door. Most would be willing to oblige as long as the rooms are available. If not, the gallant stewards can be counted on for a room swap. Just don't attempt to offer a non-smoking room to the smokers for obvious reasons. You'll get a flat 'no' in your face. The penalty for a stealth puff could amount to a couple of hundreds. Add another zero behind those figures should the nicotine stick leave an indelible souvenir on the carpet.

Most of us make it a point to inform the 'occupants' by knocking three times on the door before entering the room with a polite "Excuse me", just so that he/she/they know that we are in transit. It is followed by a quick check of cupboards, toilet and under the bed for human trespassers, before tossing the cabin baggage onto the unused twin bed. It is said that the messier the bed, the less likely we would have uninvited 'roommates'.

Not that I did. Thanks to my house-keeping habits, my bed's already less than showroom ready, to begin with.

A girlfriend refused to fly to London after the last one gave her such an unpleasant experience. With the lights off, she was about to doze off when the television screen came alive on its own accord. The tired girl struggled to locate the stray remote on the bed which she assumed was accidentally pressed on. After a few minutes of futile skimming, she reluctantly turned on the table lights, only to see the remote sitting aloof on the table.

Puzzled, she attributed it to an electrical problem, switched off the television and returned to catch up where she left off. Moments later, the screen buzzed to life again. Irritated, she decided to switch the mains off once and for all. Thus the third occurrence had her jumping out of bed and speeding to a colleague's room in her night gown. Perhaps there was a logical explanation, but it sure left a bad taste.

One of my favourite stations is an island with clear blue waters and white sandy beaches. The humble airport has no aerobridge and disembarkation is via a flight of steps ala private plane style where celebrities and politicians would descend with a perfected wave of the hand. This is the closest I could get to a dramatic entrance where I could play make believe.

The best part about the station is the transport to the resort via speedboat. We arrive in the night and most choose to crowd around on the exposed deck for the twenty minute ride. The galloping boat sends showers of salt water splashing up as it rides the waves. It is exhilarating and the constant gust of the cool night wind keeps motion sickness at bay. Thanks to the hair spray, we girls have a helmet of wind-defying hair.

The resort welcomes us with a softly lit boardwalk and crystal clear waters. The friendly staff presents a tray of drinks before dishing out the keys to the room. It is like a game of *The Weakest Link*. The unlucky person picked for THE room is unlikely to get any redress.

THE room is at the very end of a row. Each room features two backdoors, one leading to the spartan bathroom and another identical door that opens up to a stark-walled backyard with no lighting. After one too many openings of the wrong door and only to be facing a creepy blanket of pitch darkness, I would mark it to prevent another inadvertent scare.

It is well known to be favoured by a 'resident' who often treats the unsuspecting occupant to a recital of the alphabet past midnight. The sweet child-like voice on the other end of the telephone line would go "Hello, would you like to hear my ABCs?" Even as the half-asleep victim grapples with the seemingly innocent offer from a little girl, the recital would begin.

"A,B,C,D... H,I,J,K ..." the high and cutesy pitch of the voice slides to a disturbing inhumanly low and almost animal-like growl. By then, he or she will have either wet the bed or passed out. Thus, the infamous ABC room is left vacant while the girls choose to bunk in together.

In one of the Japanese hotels, the crew is allocated rooms on all floors except the third, if possible. En-route, no one brings up the subject of strange encounters of the ghostly kind. No one dares. The particular floor has its fair share of disgruntled guests who complained of disturbing sightings of what is known as the Japanese Housekeeper.

The old lady is rumoured to have been murdered by a loony guest in one of the rooms decades ago. She was savagely decapitated and stuffed under the bed. Somehow her spirit remains and continues to do what she was adept in. Those who have the luck to make her acquaintance all concluded a similar sequence of activities.

According to one account, the sudden cold brush of air across the face woke a sleeping stewardess. Her eyes opened to a faint silver-haired silhouette across the room silently bent over her duties. In fear, she shut her eyes tightly and willed the Japanese auntie to go clean another room. It seemed like hours before she opened her eyes again, only to see her seated at the corner of the dimly lit room. That was enough to set the vocal sirens off. She did a Flo-Jo and insisted to get a change of rooms at three in the morning. The hotel staff did so immediately. No questions asked.

Recently, an Indonesian stewardess shared with me an encounter in Manchester. On the way to her room after dinner, she noticed a figure leaning against the wall by the side of the hotel lobby leading to the lifts. It was a bony woman clothed in ethnic Asian attire, her head wrapped in a dark scarf. She remained motionless while the flurry of hotel guests walked past her from both directions. None threw a glance her way. Yet the woman stood out like a sore thumb. Why didn't anyone notice her? As the stewardess walked towards her, the hairs on the back of her neck stood erect. Something was not quite right, she knew. But still, that was the only way to reach the lifts. Eyes lowered to the gleaming floor, she briskly made her way there, taking care to inch as far as she could from the lone figure.

Walk, just walk. Don't look. The terrified girl told herself. The bent figure raised her head the moment she was within mere meters away. Instinctively, the stewardess raised hers as well and their eyes met. Except that instead of eyeballs, what greeted the girl was a pair of hollow black pits. Somehow the ghostly entity knew that this human had the unwelcome ability to sense her presence and wanted to make contact. Either that or it was curious to see how fast the poor girl could sprint across the lobby without wetting her panties.

Yet another steward had a disturbing experience. Unable to sleep, he tossed and turned on the overly-soft and creaky mattress. Think sleepy thoughts, he told himself. Just then, the temperature dropped several notches, bringing a sudden chill to the room. He pulled the duvet up over his chest and curled up on his side. Moments later, the other side of his bed sank lower, as though someone had laid on it. He stopped breathing and remained completely still. Again, the slight rustling of the sheets was apparent.

As much as he tried to convince himself that it was probably due to his imagination, it was impossible to ignore the movement behind his back. The bed was occupied and he was not the only one for sure. With his heart threatening to leap out of his throat, the steward sealed his eyes shut and prayed. When he next came to, it was several hours later. Not wanting to take his chances, the guy requested a change of room and made a mental note of the original room number which obviously had a 'guest' who overstayed.

There is a well circulated story about the steward who was holding fort on the upper deck of a 747, while the other two colleagues were resting in the crew bunk. A lady passenger came to the galley to request a particular cocktail, said to be her husband's favourite. She thanked him before highlighting the seat number. He did not recognize the lady but being galley-based, thought he must have missed her during the earlier supper service.

The seat was occupied by a male passenger who appeared surprised when the drink was served. "I didn't order any," he told the steward.

"But Mr. C, your wife did. She indicated that it's your favourite," he replied.

"But my wife is..." his voice trailed off. He accepted the drink, a distant look on his face.

It was later known that the passenger was indeed travelling with his wife. She was able to recline fully though - in a beautifully crafted wooden box down in the cargo hold.

Ever wonder what happens when someone dies onboard? It has happened on several occasions when an ailing heart gave up the fight. A few spent their last moments in the small confinement of the lavatory, too weak to even press the alert button. It is sad to think about how lonely and frightened they must have felt, battling the unknown, drawing the last few painful breaths while the rest of the passengers laughed and cried over their movies.

Some years back, an old man passed on in this manner and slumped against the bi-fold door, rendering it stuck from the outside. It was a long while before alarm bells sounded, after someone lost his patience on the unresponsive occupant. The stewards eventually removed the door via the hinge before they could get to the deceased. It being a full flight, they couldn't possibly place him in the original seat without freaking his neighbours out. Thus, the morbid task of settling him in the crew rest bunk - the very same bunks that we sleep in, in total pitch darkness for countless long flights. Naturally, the lower of the double bunk nearest to the entrance would be used in such circumstances - which explains why seniors would never choose that particular bunk during crew rest.

One especially eerie tale revolves around a set of crew on their way to Paris.

The first shift went for their rest in the crew bunk after the first meal service. Typically, not everyone goes at the same time. A few will take their time to linger over an extra helping of dessert, change into comfortable attire or use the lavatory. Others have unfinished duties in the cabin.

On this occasion, a handful went up to the bunk first. It was not long before the group left in haste. A steward on his way up to rest was curious to see them leave but raised no questions. He ended up alone in the 8-bedder, 2-seater bunk. Moments after drifting off to sleep, the man was rudely woken by a rough shaking of his leg. Thinking that he must have overslept and was given a wake-up call by a colleague, he sprung up. However, there was not a sign of anyone. He fumbled to find the light in the tight confines of the upper bunk, raced down the steps and bumped into the supervisor who was ready to take his rest. Not a word was breathed to him either. Male ego at play?

The spooky scene was replayed. It didn't take long for the furious supervisor to realise why he was 'lucky' enough to have his choice of bunks despite being the last one. The group was rounded up for a round of irate accusations. No one admitted that a ghostly encounter was to be blamed instead.

Fact or fiction? No one really knows. But one thing's for sure. I wouldn't be caught sleeping in the bunk alone.

Ever heard an Eurasian friend or colleague speak Mandarin? All the time. The Singaporean culture being diverse and intertwined hardly raises any brows in surprise to have our Indian friends gabbing away in Hokkien with their Chinese *kakis* (friends) over a cup of kopi-O.

But in this case of a Malay stewardess, alarm bells were ringing when she babbled in Mandarin. Legend has it that a trio of stewardesses (one Malay and two Chinese) decided to bunk in together during a layover stop in one of the Asian cities. The grand 5-star hotel houses a distinctive pair of wall-length yellow talisman in its spacious lobby.

"To ward off our *friends*."

During check-in, a cheeky steward had warned them about the presence of the unknown. "I was told that some itchy fingers touched the urn or vase on top of the T.V. and suffered disturbed sleep for the entire night. You girls can bunk in with me if you're scared," he ended with a wink.

The three junior girls smacked him on the arm playfully and swore never to bunk in with him should he be the last man on Earth. Later that night, the Malay girl tossed and turned in bed, unable to get a wink of rest. The other girls were woken by the constant shifting of her restless form and decided to stay up for a chit-chat session. The girlie interval went well when suddenly the lights went out. Screams shook the room as they scrambled to grab each other while feeling around for the light switches. When the lights came on, they found the Malay girl huddled in a corner of the room, a mop of hair over her bent knees.

"Noor, are you okay?" The two were concerned. She gave no response. Slowly, they walked towards the shivering figure. Nooraini lifted her head when they were mere steps away and that's when she started to utter Mandarin at full-speed, a language totally foreign to the girl. The other two freaked out at the sight and ran out to get help.

The version from the rumour mill has it that Nooriani stopped talking only several hours later and was so severely traumatized that she was arranged to be positioned (flown) back to base.

As for the urn, I never did get to ask her if it was a case of itchy fingers.

For me, sleep has always been a luxury, especially after a tiring service on a long-haul flight. Even if I ended up on the bunk-mortuary or checked into that dreaded room at the end of the hallway, I would be out cold in minutes. Personally, in my thirteen years of staying in hotels all over the world, I've not experienced anything out of the ordinary, and thankfully too.

In any case, I stand by an old Chinese saying :
平时不做亏心事，夜半敲门也不惊。- If you have not done anything against your conscience, fear not the knock on the door at midnight.

18

RESCUE MISSION

We used to stay in the now defunct MRM Hotel, Taipei. The gaudy coloured carpet lining the narrow, dingy corridors was an instant put-off. The rooms' musky odour of old carpet which had not seen the light of day in decades often necessitated a liberal spray of strong perfume to mask it or an outward push of its creaky windows. View? None to speak of. Unless you consider the sights of the opposite industrial buildings, funeral palour and honking traffic a visual treat.

The rooms came with two boxes of tissue, one in the bathroom and another strategically placed beside the firm bed. I was naïve enough to consider that, the saving grace of the room. It was much later when I realised that boys from my flight would receive calls from friendly strangers hoping to share the box of tissue. And it was not the one in the bathroom.

The food streets of Taipei are alluring for a 'Chinese-tongue' like me. One rainy afternoon, after rounds of Shabu Shabu, I made my way back to the hotel. A few hundred metres away from my destination, I caught sight of a dark greyish form by the corner of a pavement. As I approached, I slowly realised that it was an animal, probably a dog or overfed cat.

It was indeed a dog, an extremely dirty and frail-looking canine with the saddest eyes I have ever seen. The rain was pounding on its body and all it could do was tuck its tail between its skinny legs and shiver non-stop. The few people who walked past paid nary a scant notice. Juggling the umbrella and shopping bags, I dug out tomorrow's breakfast, a hotdog bun. Not knowing if I was a friend or foe, it backed away when I offered the bun. Moving ever so slowly, I reached out to pat its head. Dad would nag. He doesn't encourage striking friendships with strangers. It remained rooted this time but rejected my bun still.

Thoughts raced through my head. Got to get it somewhere safe and warm. But where? How?

Looking at the sorry bundle of matted fur and bones, I made up my mind. I was going to bring an illegal guest up to my room. Stuffing the contents of my bags into one, I tentatively scooped it up and raced back to the hotel. A lone security guard at the back door was dozing in cool comfort of the rain. The coast was clear. With the little fellow in my bag and shielded from sight, I tip-toed in.

Once in the safety of my room, I set about a nice, soapy warm bath for both of us. That was when I discovered the little one was a boy. He seemed to know my intentions and not once did he flinch when I ran the brush through his matted fur. He turned out to be a real beauty, a light grey Shih Tzu with huge, bright eyes. It was the first and only time I had ever shared my bed with a stranger.

As a little girl, I had been sneaking stray kittens into the house, only to be given away by their plaintive mews and resulting in a scolding from Mum. The woman often wondered aloud as to why her daughter's penchant for all things furry doesn't run in the family. She did not stop me from having two darling hamsters though, which later ran a brood of thirty. Ducklings, chicks, bunnies, doves, and terrapins pretty much made up my mini zoo.

The first bridge had been crossed but where do we go from here? I needed to get Xiao Gua a home. Leaving him in the room, I went out in search of the nearest pet clinic. No one wanted another mouth to feed. "The streets of Taiwan are full of dogs," they say. "People buy them when they're cute puppies and chuck them when the novelty's gone. There are homeless pedigrees everywhere!"

Undaunted, I went from shop to shop, clinic to clinic. My legs ached from all that walking, my toes blistered. Three hours later, I returned to the hotel without a new home for Xiao Gua.

"Xiao Gua! Xiao Gua!" I called out, expecting to see him running towards the door. He was nowhere in the room. My heart dropped and I started to panic. Don't tell me that the chambermaid came into the room when I was out? I rushed out and stopped the lady when she was just about to push her cart away. Indeed, Xiao Gua barked his lungs out after I left and the staff was alerted. In fact, he had tried to dash out when the lady opened the door to investigate.

"Please don't report this to the management. I just wanted to find him a home," I pleaded with the kind woman. I knew the penalty for breaking such rules. She had no intention to do so. In fact, she was smitten at first glance and hoped that I could allow her to be Xiao Gua's new family.

It is interesting to note how life's events turn out. The last time I visited Taipei, the familiar voice at the end of the line happily reported Xiao Gua's weight gain. And when I think of MRM Hotel, I see not the dingy room nor rundown décor, but the kind soul who took Xiao Gua in without asking for anything in return.

19

PARTY TIME

The cabin crew loves a good time. After a hectic workout onboard, it is back to the soft beds of fine hotel rooms to recharge one's batteries. While the teetotalers jostle for elbow space amid the mad sales crowd, others trawled the streets for water-holes to hydrate their soul.

The early closure of drinking joints does little to dampen their spirits. It usually means a trip to the nearest 24-hour supermarket to buy more booze, mostly six-packs. With the union flexing its negotiation muscle, most hotels pamper the airline crew with a designated crew room equipped with PCs, a fridge, java machine, TV and the occasional pool table or card games. More often than not, the room is situated at the far corner on a selected level so that the revelry makers cause minimal disturbance to other hotel guests.

I used to join my colleagues for such drinking sessions. It was fun to just relax on the carpeted floor and chill out in Abercrombie and Birkenstock garb - common crew dress code. At times, the partying would be spruced up by bottles of hard liquor, champagne and mixers.

I recall a senior supervisor whose hands would tremble

involuntarily until his next alcohol break. Behind the perpetually rosy-hued cheeks and shaky hands was a harmless old man who bothered no one and was competent in his duties. Not until one not-so-fine day when he failed to turn up for checkout at the hotel lobby. A hurried call to his room revealed that the man was zonked out between the sheets from an overnight affair with his Black Label. With the help of two stewards who practically threw all his belongings into the cabin bag, he rushed down in record time.

News from the gossip vine spread and a D.I. - Disciplinary Investigation was conducted.

I always say :

As the liquid flow, the mood mellows.

Women seem shallow, a few turn dirty fellows.

A close friend S revealed the real reason behind the breakup with her seemingly perfect boyfriend. He was not the typical Don Juan good-looker but had no problem attracting women with his boyish charms and bad-boy demeanour. The buxomly girl was not lacking in the looks department and they made an extremely cute couple.

At a Paris stopover and in their usual routine, they joined the rest for drinks in one of the stewardesses' room. Several rounds of bourbon coke and vodka limes later, some were in seventh heaven. Some stumbled their way back to their own room to puke or crash in private. Soon, only the couple and the hostess remained. Being the occasional drinker, my friend S fell victim to the alcohol racing through her bloodstream and slumped in a corner of the carpeted room. When she next came to, the rhythmic creaking of bed coils stopped in its tracks. The occupants of that bed did not include her. Shell-shocked, the girl emptied her guts right onto the shocked bastard of a boyfriend and stormed back to the room.

No words were exchanged thereafter. No action was taken by her either. I guess in her case, it is the unsaid that speaks louder.

I read with interest on another case that hit the headlines. A steward was remanded after a stewardess claimed to have been sexually assaulted by him.

Did the alcohol play accomplice? Or the irresistible allure of sweet nymphs? A misinterpretation of the girl's innocent conversation, seemingly to habour an indecent proposal perhaps? Or a case of the morning after, when the girl regrets the night's actions and cries wolf?

One thing's for sure, the company's on his back for breaking the golden rule : Do not enter a female colleague's room. Period.

In the early years, we used to enjoy the game of catching. Not the school-days version where you run around crimson-faced, tagging your taunting friends on the school field carpeted with cow grass and prickly mimosa. The adult version involved the same red-faced grown up participants in a much confined area the size of a hotel room with a blind-folded 'catcher' sending everyone packing their bods into whatever space imaginable. As one can imagine, there was not a labyrinthine of hiding places in these rooms. Its players contorted in all shapes possible to squeeze into cupboards, shelves and under the dusty bed. Still, it always brought loads of laughter when our efforts to stifle giggles and heavy breathing failed.

When extended playtime of Hide-and-Seek became too taxing for our aching bones, we would settle down for a few rounds of cards. *Chor Dai Di* (a Cantonese card game) was a favourite and an easy game to pick up. While some battled it out casino-style at one table, another table featured like-minded ones who chose not to part with their tuition fees. The penalty was usually gulping down glasses of Evian or spoonfuls of breakfast preserves. Didn't seem much of a penalty at first, but when the umpteenth glass had gone swooshing down the ready-to-burst stomach, you would feel as though the internal organs were doing a mini surf. Suddenly water didn't seem like such a great idea after all.

There are some hotels who reject cabin crew (to be fair, not just our airline) whom they claim to be too noisy, too underdressed for their image and basically too homesy. Certain thrifty individuals prepared breakfast, lunch and dinner from a trusty Sanyo traveler cook-pot, all in the comfort of their room the size of two HDB bomb shelters. Some even draped laundered panties on the lamp shades to dry and left tell-tale triangular patches on the shades.

We call this particular act, 'squatting', as it literally involves the act of dishing up culinary delights in this less-than-dignified position. A typical scenario would be a tuned up television volume coupled with the hot shower on full-blast. The former works to drown the cacophony of clinks and clanks while the latter masks overpowering smells emitting from the makeshift kitchen. Often, a vigilant lookout for chambermaids was necessary as the whiffs of Maggi curry mee (instant noodles) escaped through the gaps of the door and danced their way to the nostrils of grouchy, overworked hotel staff.

Squatting was not without its dash of fun. During wintry stays in Europe, a few colleagues cooked up a storm in one of the girls' room, sharing tips while churning the gossip mill. It didn't hurt that playing chef saved us from forking out at least thirty bucks for a plate of fried rice. The last time I dined out in Copenhagen left me forty poorer. You'll be surprised with the local cuisines they could dish out from a measly looking pot. Nasi Lemak, laksa, chicken rice… those were the days.

Hotel fire alarms seem extra sensitive nowadays. The bare trail of smoke from a single match stick could trigger the hyper-alert system, rendering squatting sessions mission impossible. Once, a mortified steward had three burly Danish men from the fire brigade threatening to knock down his door when his fried luncheon meat told on him. The guy still had the wits to discard his dinner down the toilet before wetting his hair and wrapping a bath towel around himself. He snarled in ire at being disturbed in the middle of a shower as the visitors combed the area. He demanded an explanation while hoping that the sounds from the television would drown the mad drumming of his heart.

The message was clear. Squatting days were pretty much over.

L … Is For The Way You Look At Me

20

DARLING, IT'S NO FLING

Hands up for those hot-blooded males who have been served by our lovely ladies and not once had a less-than-innocent fantasy about the uniform-clad feminine form. Especially when you happen to catch an eyeful of breast when they bend to lower your shades. How about a show of leg when the skirt flaps open inadvertently or the curve of the rear comes within your vision when the beautiful host arches her back to close the overhead compartment?

Come on. Not once? Even female passengers appreciate how the female silhouette is accentuated.

The bolder ones attempt small talk, hoping to ease a contact number out of their desired target at the end of the pickup conversation. Some are genuinely interested in striking meaningful friendships which hopefully, could blossom into something fruitful. Others display their agendas almost point-blankly.

A sure turn off is the constant puffing up of one's financial chest by trumpeting the latest flashy wheels, private yacht or Nassim Hill bungalow. I remember a First Class passenger who could not stop boasting about his lap pool and garage of fast cars. While I was being polite to acknowledge his health of wealth, I could not help but look at him in a different light.

A shady one, that is. When the weasel-looking man kept hinting that he was looking for a lady to complete his home, I knew it was time to excuse myself on the pretext of being engaged with other duties. Complete his home? Yeah, right. More like adding the final touches to his waterbed. He slipped me a note and a personal number. I never did call. Who knows how many susceptible girls he had lured to his lair, only to use and abuse until the next one catches his fancy?

After a turnaround flight to Hong Kong, a call from the office surprised me. Not a complaint, I hoped. Short flights put us in the jeopardy zone more than long haul, as the time constraint and full load factor often cause minor lapses in service; which in the eyes of some not-so-understanding passengers are catastrophic. It turned out that a gentleman had called the Hong Kong office to ask for my contact details.

"Mr. X said that he forgot to return your pen," the lady at the other end of the line explained.

"Pen? What pen? I didn't lend anyone any pen," I replied.

"Hmm … that's strange. He insisted in getting your details so that he could deliver it from Hong Kong. Said it was a Mont Blanc and that he had to ensure that you received it."

The clouds in my head cleared. This was not a case of returning my personal item. It was more of a passenger wanting to get up close and personal with me. This particular gentleman had earlier enquired about a Mont Blanc pen from the in-flight sales catalogue and he seemed to be particularly interested in me. I laughed and requested the generous gentleman be barred from accessing my details.

It does not take a rocket scientist to fish out information about hotel locations during conversations with the crew. Again, it does not take bionic eyes to zoom in on the name tag of the love or lust interest. Put one and one together and viola, the hotel phone starts ringing off the hook the minute she steps out of her stockings.

Sometimes, innocent small talk or gestures are misread and blown out of proportion. An Asian airline was hurled into the limelight for the wrong reasons. The case involving a high profiled oil tycoon, a feisty wife and a slap on a stewardess made the curious public sit up in anticipation of whatever juicy inside scoops it held. The entire cabin crew family could not stop talking about it.

Two schools of speculation : The insecure wife had let jealousy gotten the better of her. In a rash moment of disdain for a sweet young thing, she responded physically. In this instance, the poor lass played the part of innocent victim whose only crime was to be in her prime. Ok, so the subtle peek-a-boo display of creamy flesh didn't help either.

But others argued. What if, just what if... this particular husband had a history of sorts not worth reiterating in public? Surely, it must have taken more than just a possible flash of flesh and friendly banter to incur a wife's wrath? Had she tipped her tolerance scale over an extended period of playing dumb to her husband's activities?

It's anyone's conjuncture. What's tickling the crew's interest lies in the fat cheque issued to the stewardess.

"That girl's so lucky to *kena* the right combination. Rich man, jealous wife, stupid enough to deliver a slap to her face instead of the husband," my girlfriend Y commented wistfully when I probed her for juicy details. "I want to select my paxs for PR (small talk) very carefully next time."

"Why? Afraid of being the next victim?" I teased.

"No man," she continued. "I want to be slapped! Then I can sue her panties off and quit flying! Ha ha ha!"

Indeed, that will be a joke among the girls for a long time to come. For some, I really think they meant it. A slap followed by a fat cheque. Hmmm... that may very well deserve a clap. As for enterprising Y, she's gearing up on her honey trapping skills and not giving up hope.

There are plenty of stories about girl meets rich businessman passenger, falls in love (with his fat account) and out of favour within a year. Of course, not all men are out to pull a fast one on our girls. Likewise, the pretty stewardess who just accepted your dinner invitation might genuinely be interested to know more about you.

If sparks flies and the wood catches fire, good for you. If not, retreat. At times when an overzealous suitor refuses to take no for an answer, it becomes a violation of personal space.

Just a warning to men with dubious agendas. Respect all women as you would your mother. You should, in case you don't. The cabin crew leads a glamorous lifestyle and most of us are a friendly bunch who enjoy some harmless fun. That does not equate loose morals. It's wonderful if boy meets girl and falls in love eventually, but if you come onto us for very wrong reasons, back off!

I believe one commands respect, not demand it. Likewise, in the case of the love game, while being financially comfortable does chock up more bonus points in your lady love's checklist, it is by no means the main deciding factor to influence her opinion of you. Most of us are in search of a soul mate who can provide a reasonably comfortable life. Only the rare few are simply seeking a fat meal ticket out.

That said, those interested in the latter - flash your rocks, fancy watches and promise them the mansion. Enjoy it while it lasts. Chances are, it is going to be as temporal as your monogamous nature.

21

Out Of Sight, Out Of Mind

D o you subscribe to the saying? In the late eighties, when flights took off on a lower frequency, a trip to the US could mean 14-16 days without touching base. During those days, when Honolulu was still viable, the crew had a field time toasting for days on the sunny beaches before packing their bags for home.

The Bangkok-Paris pattern was a favourite. It made a three-day stopover in Bangkok, a shopping and feasting haven for both men and women alike. Throw in dirt cheap massages , booze and nimble pole-twirling girls clad in less-than-generous fabric and there you have it.

Thai paradise.

Even the alternatively-lifestyled males are not left out of the party. Check out the high numbers of paired up male passengers on Bangkok routes. The pint-sized hair maestro of a well-known salon is a regular, though his male companions seem to change as often as his expensive wardrobe.

Some of our colleagues took to the lease of freedom like bees to honey. It drove them wild. It was not uncommon for them to organise a private party at a new waterhole to drink the night away or lounge in the hottest clubs, rubbing shoulders with the beautiful crowd. One steward called Guo Ren one night, inviting him to his room.

"What's up, bro?" He was curious.

The answer caught him by surprise. Our friend here had asked for some lady companionship; the appearance of not one, but two purring she-kittens made him decide to call Guo Ren over to help lighten the load.

"Very solid bodies! Real melons! You've got to see them. Two is cheaper, the agency said. We can split the bill bro," the highly excited guy said breathlessly over the phone.

"No thanks bro, you can enjoy them both. I'll take a rain check." Guo Ren feigned an exaggerated yawn. I remember teasing him about the lost golden opportunity when he related the incident to me. On the inside, I was not half as nonchalant as I tried to appear. I do trust him. I mean, I wanted to and needed to. We saw each other once or twice per month, treasuring the short moments we had on common days off.

Men are animals, predators who hunt to satisfy their needs. Needless to say, the thrill of the hunt adds to that. At least, that was what I used to hear from victims of failed relationships. Would he tire of me one day, I wonder? My infectious laughter that he loves, would he liken it to that of a hyena's some day? The body that brought him endless visual pleasure, would my womanly curves fail to ignite desire in time to come? Each time I looked deeply into his earnest eyes, I wanted to believe that we were in for the long haul.

As the months went by after graduation, we saw less of each other as rosters clashed. Despite the fatigue and jet-lag after each flight, we struggled to make every minute last.

The first two years were trying. During then, the number of flight swaps was limited to less than ten a year. After exhausting our lifelines, the only thing we could do was to hope that each roster hailed good news. More often than not, we ended up disappointed. Looking back, I realise that I was so caught up in this whirlwind of love and courtship that I had neglected the existence of my family. I had given first priority to dating, kicking them back to a far second.

As opportunities to meet abated, so did the yearning in our hearts. Conversations somehow dried up. The familiar voice at the end of the line struggled for words to fill in the awkward silence. Stories we had initially found entertaining now failed to rouse our interest. The daily flurry of emails that used to greet each other eventually dwindled to almost a crawl. The scariest part of it all is, knowing a problem obviously exists but not having the solution to it. What happened? How could a relationship that seemed so right end up terribly wrong? When my promotion letter came, the first people I shared the news with was my family, not Guo Ren. Suddenly, the message was clear. We once treaded the shared path. Not anymore. Amicably, we hugged each other one last time before going our separate ways.

22

THE DATING GAME

Outstations? Hardly. It takes a lot more than Cupid to allow strangers within close proximity while in a foreign land. For the few who found love in an unfamiliar setting, the long distance relationships can be trying. Take my batch mates for example. Many arrived in Singapore, wide-eyed and innocent. The initial months were difficult, to say the least. If being home-sick wasn't enough to induce tears, try coupling that with love-sickness. Hard-earned days off are spent crossing the causeway to Malaysia, only to share what limited time with the family, friends and the better half. In the days before budget airlines, air travel was costly, often amounting to hundreds of dollars which could pay two months' rent. After a while, the strain took its toil; boyfriends staged their protests. Now what did they expect the girls to do? Quit before the bond was up and return to their hometown after a long, anticipative wait to realise a dream of flying?

Moulded by the environment; within a year or two, these young girls grow up in more ways than one. Personalities and ideals reshape. Especially those from more rural settings, exposure to an exciting world of glamour, brands and luxury leads to the gradual drifting away from their childhood sweethearts.

Bro used to quiz me about airline girls. Are most of them attached and super high maintenance, he wondered. His friend had complained after the third Gucci bag demanded by his stewardess girlfriend. Indeed, the spending habits of some of them are far from petty. Blame it on the culture vultures. Still, like mum always says, 不能一竹竿打翻整船人: we can't use a single bamboo stick to knock the occupants off a boat at one go. There is no single yardstick for every case.

Likewise for our girls. External appearances and spending lifestyles aside, many of us are looking for what every other girl wants - a romantic, sensitive, pleasant looking, sincere and importantly, faithful man to love. One who not only loves us but those around us. Is that so difficult to find? Blind dates are turned down or set up depending on how the guys perceive stewardesses to be. In the dating game, misconceptions of stewardesses are aplenty. Like the impression of us girls being vain pots or worse still, 'air pots'. Our guys don't have it easy as well; they are often saddled with the wrongful label of being too playful to stay faithful.

The doctor at our regular airport clinic was one eligible target. However, word got around that he hooked up with a very beautiful China-born stewardess. They made quite a handsome pair, I must say. Many were disappointed on the other hand. My single and very available buddy Y was no exception.

"The doc was a good catch. Nice personality, pleasant features to match… and did I mention that he is a doctor?" She lamented her lack of fortune, staring wistfully at the group of powdered Japanese ladies at the Gucci DFS. The slim and pretty lass with lustrous TV-commercial worthy tresses, has had little luck with men. Or rather, the right men.

They come with the wrong agenda, she laments. People are

attracted to her for the wrong reasons. After being turned down, one shameless loser had the cheek to ask her to introduce "any pretty stewardess" to him instead. In fact, she feels inclined to hide her occupation during initial dates in order to sieve out the potential ones. None so far, unfortunately. How do you explain to your dates that you don't do weekends, am available at odd hours of the day or go M.I.A. for 7-9 days on end?

Another friend in the IT industry chipped in his cents' worth. "With all the passengers to choose from, I'm sure there aren't many single and available stewardesses left."

On the contrary, there are. It is no wonder actually. Precious days off aside, the rest of their days are spent up in the air with nary a chance to really meet someone. Much less, connect.

While it's true that we are 'spoilt for choice' in that sense, but time-constraining meal services hardly create the ideal setting for banter. Even when either party indicates interest, some would question if this action has been cut-and-pasted onto other potential targets. Does this passenger pass his contacts to every pretty stewardess? Is she bombarded with date offers on every flight? Does agreeing to meet up mean anything?

My two cents worth of advice to our eligible men; married ones please stay away indefinitely! Play your game as you would practice *Tai Chi*. Its fluid movements hinge on the right timing and appropriate amount of strength used. Test the waters, play on your own strengths, remain genuine and sincere and refrain from charging like a beast. Strike up an intriguing conversation and suavely withdraw with a name card. If she likes what she has seen so far, she will know that a possible love connection is just a call away.

The perceived notion that stewardesses are nothing more than trophy girlfriends stood in the way of Samantha's shot at finding love. A close friend, she prefers to find love outside the confines of the cabin. The tall and attractive girl of Chinese-Indian parentage chose to let doubts cloud her better sense when a passenger courted her. The British neurosurgeon seemed sincere enough, but the thought of their first meeting being that on the plane with her in uniform, was enough to activate the 'no' button.

When their paths crossed the second time, he approached her again, only to be politely rejected. I was puzzled. Samantha had often envied the wives of successful professionals. So why do the backward cha-cha now?

"Do you even like the man in the first place?" I queried.

"I do. He cracks me up. But the place and timing are so wrong. How do I know if he likes me for who I am, and not who he thinks I am?" She sighed. Go for it, I pushed. "I mean, you are not going to marry the guy. Well, not just yet anyway. What harm can a meal do?"

From our last conversation, I suspect that she would have done things differently with hindsight. Time and tide have passed her; so has the heart of the eligible neurosurgeon - they met again, this time a little happy family greeted her.

23

MAKING LOVE OUT OF
NOTHING AT ALL

"Ten o'clock. Outside Zouk. Don't be late, woman!" Y's voice sounds high pitched whenever she is in a hurry. She never addresses me by my name. Neither do I. The girl was probably off to some manicure session. Late as usual. This is the one thing we have in common. It is a wonder how both of us manage to turn up for flights on the dot.

She was in a drinking mood and insisted that I follow. Time to move on with your life, she said. Can't stick to a 'flight-home-flight-home' routine. I did not resist. After all, it had been two years since my last party night. The dresses in my wardrobe stared back at me. Should I vamp up or go au naturel? A call from Y's mobile confirmed the dress code. Let's go demure tonight, she suggested. Long dresses, minimal war paint. No killer stilettos, nothing loud.

That night, we gave each other the once over and I let out a low whistle. "Sui! (Gorgeous)" I gave my approval of her white number with a flowy helm. Her stomach was an absolute chopping board, flat and taut without the masculine pack of abs. Consciously, I sucked in my tofu tummy and pulled at the fabric crunching up at the sides. "Aiyah, very pretty already la," she teased.

The scene had not changed much. The place was packed as usual. Heads turned wherever we went. Men stared while their lady companions glared. We eventually squeezed into a corner, stole a couple of stools from unattended tables and settled down to the mood. Small talk was almost impossible as we ended up screaming inaudibles into each other's ears. After a jug of Long Island Tea, we were dancing in our seats, tossing our heads back, attacking unknowing by-standers with a lash of freshly-washed hair.

It's funny how alcohol releases one's inhibitions. But I knew my limits then. No more Wild Coyote moves on the table. How freaking embarrassing!

"Let's play the matchstick game!" Y leaned over and yelled. I nodded. I enjoy this game. A boy I was dating back in university introduced it to me. It was a simple game of piling up the sticks one by one, creating a little shaky structure. The player who crashes the structure, loses. It was made challenging when the effects of alcohol came into play.

Y's hand was shaking slightly. On the third consecutive penalty drink, she started to waver. I was still going strong, knowing that the trick to this game entails a certain level of nonchalance. The more cautious you are, the higher the chances of knocking them flat.

An arm came in between us and placed a matchstick on the top successfully. We looked up in surprise at the gatecrasher. He smiled. Cute. We didn't attempt to empty our jug on him. And so, I took on a new player, leaving Y to pick up a couple of tips while her saviour pitted his skills against me.

The guy is good at this, I thought, as the odds started to work against me. I downed the last of my Long Island and signaled for a truce. No point getting all drunk and pukey. Besides, I reckoned he probably needed a chance to chat Y up. Or shout, in this case.

We didn't chase him away for the fact that he looked totally harmless. And friendly. And cute. Besides, there wasn't much to do other than drink, dream and drink again. When we finally decided that our lungs have had their lifetime fill of smoke and we badly needed to pee, I got off from the stool, pulling Y with me.

"Can I give you girls a lift home? I'm just about to leave," Cute Guy (CG) offered. Neither of us had asked for his name.

We looked at each other, went away for a small discussion before accepting his offer. Y argued that he seemed genuinely nice, and that none of us were high. And that he's cute. So that tipped the scales in his favour. Taking down the plate number of his metallic grey coupe, we slipped in for a quiet and relaxed ride back.

Y alighted first, with the 'subtle' hint that she will call my cell phone to check in half an hour's time. Silence between two strangers prompted an effort to make small talk. It quickly progressed to easy conversation. We delved into many topics I would not imagine sharing with someone I had just met at a club. The quirky sense of humour in him had me laughing away. As tears collected at the corner of my eyes, I realised how long I had not laughed. It felt as though a part of me was kept under the flower pot, emerging after a prolonged period in the damp, dark hibernation.

When Y's call came, we were already at the gate.

"Back in one big piece, woman. Now go wash up and *tidoh* (sleep)," I assured her. Did CG ask for my number, she wanted to know.

"Why would he?" I played dumb.

"Coz he wouldn't have been so nice as to play chauffer if he wasn't interested in one of us. And since he sent me back first … not obvious enough ah?" she reasoned.

I laughed. I was in a light mood. And yes, he left with a new number in his contact list.

CG was from a reputable law firm, though he looked nothing like a lawyer. The tanned and tall man sported a head of sun-streaked hair and an earring. When he went shirtless for the first time, I was surprised to see we had something else in common. The love of ink. His right arm bore cascading snakes while the left, a calligraphic Chinese character.

"More like a diver," Y used to comment, "and a bad boy too."

Indeed, the man had a certain impish demeanor about him. The type that parents would advise their daughters to leave outside the gate. His habit of winking while curling a lopsided smile didn't help either. Not that I cared. By the end of the tenth date, I was ready to take my chances. I was smitten.

Yes, even if he is a lawyer.

My mode of transport has changed again. Not that I had reason to complain. CG insisted on sending me to work in his collection of wheels. The man had a weakness for fast cars. "How many cars DO you have? You need a stable for these! " I couldn't suppress my curiosity, when he pulled up in the third different car that month.

He said nothing and kissed me squarely on the lips, much to my dismay as I was in uniform. I sighed, got onto the Beemer and reclined the seat. I was pooped as always after a battle onboard. Flashy wheels or not, I just wanted to get home to give my legs a much needed warm soapy soak.

If folks suspected that I was in the dating scene again, they indicated nothing. Mum held me by the arm as I was leaving the house one day. "Protect yourself," was all she said.

"I will." I looked at the permanent arch between her knitted brows and gave an assuring nod before running out to the waiting car.

It would take a blind person to not notice the extra effort I made to dress up. I would often return just before the midnight curfew, bubbly and chatty with gifts in hand. Courtesy of CG, of course. I had never probed, the obscene amount he probably earned was evident in the gifts and meals he lavished on me. Meals were always in a classy setup. The generous pampering of Tiffany trinkets, Prada bags and a pretty diamond studded Cartier watch was flattering, but it was the little gestures of cards stuffed inconspicuously among the luggage that gave me the greatest motivation to smile. Reading every line of his hand written cards helped bridge the distance between us when I was away on long hauls.

There were days when I lazed around waiting for him to knock off from work. By then, I was already hours from the next flight. Another entire day wasted. That made whatever little time we had to meet up even more precious. I became a regular on the 'Change of Flights' board, giving preferred sectors away in exchange for a weekend off. The singles would grab those.

It is after all, a world of demand and supply. Weekends off come with a hefty tag. Those wanting to earn more would sacrifice rest over higher allowances while the lovesick would trade-in most willingly. We have colleagues who squeeze every possible day off into an opportunity of extra income. That is, without infringing on flight rules which stipulates a mandatory rest interval. I know a steward who cramps two long-haul flights to New York in a month. Flights longer than eighteen hours are rewarded with an attractive in-flight allowance.

"Gotta save up for wedding," he replied when I wondered how he survives the flights. One is draining enough, but two in a row? A fat pay slip is expected, but not without its drawbacks - leaving him little time with his bride-to-be. He justified that the short term sacrifice was worth the while. Similarly, like some time-deprived, guilt-ridden parents who shower their kids with gifts, he too tries to make up for his absence with overseas purchases.

As a stewardess, the odd hours of waking at three in the morning and having breakfast at night is the norm. Sitting down to a family meal, going to the movies with the whole gang are simple luxuries; worse still if your group of friends are from the airline. Differing flight rosters render common days off a rarity. Imagine the challenge in rounding up the whole lot for a wedding dinner when half the airline guests fail to swap for days off.

Out of thirteen, I had managed only three Chinese New Year reunion dinners with the family. It is emotionally hard on the crew when festive celebrations are held thousands of miles away from their loved ones. The airline cushions this by throwing lavish buffet dinners at the hotel, where homesick members dress up, drink up and revel in the celebratory mood for a while.

An irregular lifestyle is not without its advantages though. Any day of the week can be a possible day off at the spa or movies. Shoe enthusiasts can be first in line for the Nine West warehouse sale on Friday mornings before the rest of Singapore goes wild the next day. Nothing beats running errands and shopping on weekdays with the whole of Orchard Road to yourself. Especially for someone like me – strangely enough, out of uniform, I am a social hermit. The less human interaction, the better.

Like any colleague in the dating scene, it is a struggle to make time after a horrendously draining flight. Imagine waking up the night before, a couple hours spent on preparation, transportation and reporting in, working through twelve hours, then back again after touch down for a quick shower and off to the arms of your beau. I wanted to look my best still after near twenty waking hours. The skin can do its breathing later. Slapping foundation onto my face, I threw all beauty caution to the wind. Nature has its ways of retaliating; my freckles now trace the Milky Way.

Initially the excitement of seeing CG dulled the effects of fatigue;

consequently, the adrenaline ran dry and I succumbed to it. After a long day out at the movies, restaurants and the final pit stop at his place, I was ready to crash. In fact, I drooled through most part of each blockbuster.

A colleague faced similar issues with her husband who clocks regular hours in the office. The couple had been married for four years and she confided that of late, their bedroom activities were a tad more thrilling than that of the pandas. The tight frequency of flights and a hyperactive, precocious toddler had sapped the energy out of her petite frame. Her in-laws were more than happy to dump Junior back the moment she returned from flight. It didn't help that work kept her husband away until supper time. Sometimes she would be woken late at night, only to feel a familiar tugging at her nightie. Contrary to passionate movie scenes, that is not exactly the most arousing act when sleep is of priority.

"But a man needs to release," she told me resignedly. With that in mind, the weary woman allowed the ardent worshipper into her sacred temple late after opening hours.

It didn't help that she is a light sleeper. Even the smallest movement would wake her. On days with late night or early morning departures, breakfast together was out of the question. In fact, he was accustomed to having a breakfast partner in the form of the morning papers. It was not long before trivial tiffs graduated to a seven point rating on the Richter scale. In a fiery outburst, he accused his wife of being "like a dead fish in the water". That must have hurt, to be likened to a fish floating belly up when the very same man once dropped his jaw at the sight of her naked body years ago. Eventually, both graduated to sleeping in separate rooms.

"It is only a matter of time before he loses all interest in me." Looking at her moistened eyes when she related her pain and loss of direction, I could only provide a listening ear and hoped that I would not end up another sorry statistic. Who am I to counsel on bedroom matters when I was only but in the rudimentary stage?

Work took CG away on trips as well and at times, we went for weeks without seeing each other. He made up for it by special deliveries of champagne roses with Godiva to my room; God, I never knew chocolates tasted this heavenly. Not wanting to devour them at one sitting, I would pack the little delights to share with the other sweet tooth in the household : Mum. I grew up on Cadbury milk and nuts and have been a loyal customer of this 'happy fuel'. Mum used to steal bites and was careless enough to leave teeth marks on them. Fake an accusation on her and the petite woman would insist that she was sharing my guilt in consuming the caloric sin. Yeah, right.

As for the roses, I would tear out the pretty peach petals and toss them into my tub for a luxuriant soak amid lavender candle lights. It felt wonderful to be pampered, to be pursued. More so, by the one you fancy.

By the sixth month, I couldn't help but entertain a nagging thought that ran circles in my head. Was CG serious about me? If so, why haven't I met his folks yet? The men I've dated in the past clamoured to bring me back to their place, where what seems like three generations would ogle at their boy's date. I have Mum to thank for the demure, girl-next-door looks. At sixty, the mature beauty is still my dad's pride and love. Both were most particular about the proper mannerisms a young lady should display. I did not disappoint. By end of the evening, most would be eating out of my hand, and the family heirloom pushed into my refusing hands. Well, almost!

An article from a woman's magazine advised against popping the question. Not in the first stage anyway. First stage? I considered writing to the columnist with regards to her definition. Does half a year come within that range, even though it is riddled with hasty dates and longer dry spells? Does being intimate earn a girl automatic entry into the guy's home? By then, CG and I were doing more than admire the intricate tattoos of each other's body. Besides, I held the keys to his posh apartment at Grange Road.

I decided to play the waiting game. Not that there was a need to hurry anyway. It was just that the tables were somewhat turned this time and I was the one bursting with suspense. Y was never too encouraging when we first started, but seeing how he had brought me out of my hermit shell made her think twice about stating her two cents worth.

"Just be careful woman. Don't give too much, too soon." She frowned when yet another delivery of Victoria Secrets came. After all, his outward appearance did justify what every mother would warn their daughter about. I know she meant well, but part of me refused to heed her words. What is the use of holding back when it means not being able to discover what promises lie ahead? Another thought occurred to me. What if Y was jealous? After all, she was kind of into him initially. More so, now that he has proven to fill the criteria of a cute, humorous man with a fat wallet. Feeling guilty of harbouring such unkind thoughts, I quickly brushed them aside and gleefully opened the lightly scented box with pink satin ribbons.

Being away from him for weeks on end did not help allay worries of him falling prey to other women. He was the typical babe magnet and I wasn't always around to neutralize any potential attraction. Again, I bottled my doubts. And he never once questioned the potential suitors I meet in the course of work. Somehow the heart and mind could not quite agree; the latter played a mean game of the devil's advocate, wreaking havoc in my head with images of beautiful women clinging to his tanned and lean body. It didn't help when an old favourite was playing on the in-house radio – 'Who's Holding Donna Now?'

As I was relishing the courtship moments, it dawned on me that CG had been doing the giving, but something was missing, he has yet to give me a sense of security.

Perhaps I should have voiced my thoughts. Two months after our first anniversary, I left on a London flight. The man gave me a lingering kiss when the traffic light turned red near the airport, smudging my carefully lined lips.

"I'll miss you," he said. Three simple words that was music to my ears.

Good fortune shone on me when I was activated for an earlier return flight. I was elated. Most of us would have bitched as an early callback means a loss of shopping opportunities and allowances. When I touched down in Singapore, I texted him, ending it "With love, from London." I was all tingling with excitement, the thought of springing a surprise on him wrestled with the urge to call him.

The maid shook her head. No, her sir was not at home. That's strange, I thought. His three babies were in the stables, so where could he have gone to? His slippers were missing from the rack, I noticed; but of course, the pool where he does a mean fifty laps daily to maintain that sun-kissed tan. I thanked the maid before making my way down. Squinting under the glare of the relentless sun, I scanned the area under the roof of my palm.

Then, my heart dropped. There he was, the unmistakable physique with the tattoos. The very same corner of the pool where we had our clandestine workout after lights out. Only this time, the cascading snakes on his arm disappeared partially around the waist of another woman. I couldn't make out her features, but her honey-tan and supple full figure told me that this she-bitch was no slacker in the looks department either.

I swallowed hard to quell the lump in my throat. Part of me wanted to march up to deliver my own surprise. Another part pulled hard at the emotional reins. Why start an ugly scene over such a man, if he really is one in the first place? I turned and ran, not caring that people turned to stare at this girl doing a sprint with hot tears flowing freely.

Call me stupid, but I ended the relationship on an unusually amicable note. CG pressed on for the reason. What has he done wrong? I was surprised he had the cheek to even ask. But of course, he had no inkling that I already seen through his sweet pampering gestures and clever jokes. In fact, I had seen more than I bargained for. Enough was enough.

You are not the one for me, I told him squarely in the face when we met over lunch a day later. For a split second, a flicker of guilt flashed across his face and he swiftly composed himself. Not wanting to stay a minute longer, I pushed the bags of previous gifts towards him and left with my head held high, my heart numb in the pits.

24

DID YOU MEAN IT WHEN
YOU SAID 'I DO'?

I was lunching with some ex-colleagues at a coffee joint the other day and the animated conversation revolved around sex in the cities. While the convenience of a cushy five-star hotel room in exotic countries does up the thrill factor, it by no means changes the fact that a sexual tryst constitutes betrayal.

Most colleagues who partake in such clandestine carnal interactions take great pains to do it behind closed doors. These discreet affairs, like plots in a mini soap, rarely escape the keen eyes of the crew though. A nanosecond exchange of flirty glances or a light deliberate brush of skin against skin. It is often a case of self-disclosure through excessive attempts to cover up. Nobody wants the reputation of being a 'tryer' (skirt chaser) or be labeled a 'bicycle' (I'll leave you to work this one out). Often its lead characters had their better halves kept in the dark.

The news that hogged the headlines and drove evening tabloids into a frenzy, also set the airline crew's tongues a-wag. An ordinary-looking steward, his young wife and a foreign mistress. The latter had been harassed by the Taiwanese mistress, who taunted the svelte mother of two, throwing her into deep depression after the lousy man of a husband did nothing to deny his wrongdoings. The vamp herself was married to a captain who had not doubted the wife's fidelity. After repeated suicidal threats went unheeded, the shattered wife threw herself down from their unit, days short of her next birthday. Shortly after, the mistress left the country as she could no longer bear the weight of accusations.

I knew none of them personally. A colleague who was a mutual friend hurled a string of profanity at the man. He sat quietly defeated, at a table farthest from the deceased, after a beating by the brother-in-law earlier.

I would like to think that for every discontented man who wanders to lush pastures, there remain a thousand more faithful stayers. In the airline, the prolific players who kept straying to other women's panties are few and far between.

One of them, a high-flier in his 30s, is a tall and swanky man who was a former gym instructor. His charms are apparent and he is well aware of the women drawn to him. They make no excuse for hovering around the handsome man with chiseled features, often slapping his bulging biceps coyly and sending come-hither signals across.

His wife used to be a stewardess before she quit to start her brood of four kids. The petite, demure woman was pleasant-looking but certainly no competition for the pack of coquettish she-wolves. What surprises me is the openness of his friendly affairs with them, despite knowing how rapidly the rumor mill churns out the 'Extra, extra, read all about it!'

Of late, a tall, striking stewardess emerged leader of the pack and claimed the dangling rights to his beefy arm. The attractive girl actively swapped flights in order to fly with her man and before long, the entire airline crew was abuzz with the latest development of their sexual rendezvous.

Was I ever one of his conquests? I was after all, his type, the team girls used to tease. Certainly, there were sure-fire signals coming from him when we worked together in First Class. He would stand closer than necessary while we prepared cocktails, so much so that I could feel the hairs on the nape of my neck swaying under the weight of his breath. The proximity of an attractive man trying to navigate towards me did make my heart skip a beat. I looked down on the galley top, not daring to draw in any more air than I could. Fearing that he could hear the erratic drumbeat resonating within the cavity of my barely moving chest, I scooped up the drinks and headed for the cabin, deliberately breaking the moment.

Nay, I disappointed them. I was a one-man woman and he was not one to shit in his own backyard.

When will news finally reach the ears of his wife? For some time, he panicked when she contemplated resuming her flying career as that spelt the end of his wandering days. Luck decided to smile on him a while longer. Her application was rejected. As to how long our friend would continue sowing his wild oats, I guess I'll just wait for updates from the F4 gossip vine.

Recently, I was at Takashimaya shopping for infant clothes intended for a baby shower. As I was going down the escalator, I locked eyes for a split second with a senior steward I used to respect. I had flown with him and his lovely dimple-cheeked wife, who is a supervisor in her early forties. Each left pleasant impressions. They had been trying in vain for a child during their many years of marriage and had even sought advice from me with regards to adoption options. The soft-spoken man doted on his wife, showering her with gifts and tender gestures.

He was ascending, an arm tightly locked around the slim waist of a girl half his age. I had a rude shock to see the sweet young thing (a Korean stewardess whom I recognized) cooing into his ears while his arms coiled around her bare-midriff. He froze just as I looked away.

Sigh… not you too. The perfect gentleman, the epitome of a loving husband.

Suddenly, I lost the mood for shopping.

Emily, a fair-skinned and doe-eyed stewardess from my team five years ago, was in a long-term relationship with a steward. The two Malaysians rented a condominium unit in the east and frequently hosted wine parties and the occasional poolside barbeques. She was not particularly beautiful but her boyfriend practically placed her on a pedestal. The lucky lass never had to lay a manicured finger around the house. Partaking in household chores was unheard of. Every time she came back from her flight, the house would be spotless "for the arrival of my princess", as the boyfriend always put it. A vase of her favourite tiger lilies would not fail to take centre stage on the dining table. Even her panties would be laundered and tucked neatly into little folds of the lingerie drawer - part of the customized walk-in wardrobe for her personal use. The man sweated it out in the kitchen while she watched the latest Taiwanese soap in the comfort of the air-conditioned bedroom. He would de-shell each prawn and slice whatever meat into bite-sized morsels before settling down to enjoy his own food.

Oh and how he worked hard to please her in bed.

Emily confided in me that he had developed impressive tongue muscles that could go on for ages.

"Oh please, spare me the details!" I was squeamish and shy to discuss bedroom activities.

"Never bare too much to your man", she always believed. "I make it a point to be naked only in bed. It keeps them hungry."

I did a mini survey among male colleagues and proved her wrong. The visual vultures want skin. Lots of it. Period.

Two years later, Emily was swept into the arms of a divorced steward whose ex-wife used to be a beauty queen. The boyfriend was shattered. The last I heard was that she gave birth to a pair of twins and isn't as pampered by her current beau. I guess she still could enjoy her Taiwanese soaps. If she had time between chores to install a 14-inch in the kitchen, that is.

Three years ago, a colleague suddenly announced his divorce. His wife, an ex-stewardess left to realise her dream of opening an ice cream palour. Ice confection of exotic flavours were all the rage and soon, she started a successful branch in town. They were one of the best-looking couples in the airline, both active volunteers at the SPCA. We were all taken by surprise by his adamant stand on the divorce. What happened? It was one of those sad cases of cheater bugs caught in the act. In her case, it was with her panties down - an evening romp in the matrimonial bed with a useless bloke who bolted when the husband came home a day earlier. Outwardly, he wore the cuckold hat well, dealing it with a swift, decisive blow. Even as the wife tugged at his legs, begging for forgiveness. It was a moment of folly, she pleaded. His heart bled to see the person he once held dearest, now on her knees, at his total mercy. The swirl of thoughts in his throbbing head - Why? When?

Months after, he started having self doubts. Was he away too often, neglecting the needs of the wife? Why had he not noticed the extra attention she paid to his rosters and certain portions highlighted by her? Had he not flown back earlier, how long would he be kept in the dark? At times, he wondered if ignorance would have been bliss; at least, he would still have her.

I was catching up with a few friends from another airline. Amid gossips and laughs, some juicy stories were spilled. Jason, a senior flight attendant in his forties, shared his early encounter with a senior stewardess who asked him to her room. "We need to go through your check report," she said. As a greenhorn in those days, it was a matter of following instructions. Imagine his surprise when the door opened up to reveal a scantily clad colleague who wanted more than just clever conversation. So what happened then, I pressed on.

The boyish looking man simply winked before throwing me a line, "Well, let's just say that my check report was way above average."

I was not convinced and nosed around for more information from Dan, the good-looker among the thorns. He confirmed it. The man with a charming lone dimple on the left cheek had attracted his fair share of women. Obviously, not only the women were sold. When his senior steward welcomed Dan into his room in his full gear of Calvin Klein undies and Garfield slippers, he froze at the door before beating a hasty retreat. Geez, I wonder if that happens in my airline as well.

Amid all the gossips and scandalous affairs, there are stories of true love and life's second chances.

A girlfriend recently held her second wedding in Bali. The divorcee with sole custody of a bright four year-old son found love once again when she did a Zurich flight with a strapping Malay steward a year earlier. She used to lament half-jokingly that her market value was on the slide as she reaches her big four zero.

"Some more, buy one, get one free," she self-deprecated as she lost hope of finding the right father figure to complete the family portrait again.

We spoke over MSN (instant messaging) and shared the joy of her pregnancy. Over the past few months, the hormonal changes triggered many uncalled-for outbursts. The patient hubby bore the brunt of her tirade but lost it when her unreasonable accusations broke the last straw. She felt like an old, fat and ugly sow and had resented that the neighbours' daughter smiled at him.

"At us, not at me!" He threw his arms up in resignation. "I know you are going through a difficult pregnancy now but you have to understand that I married you because you are you! I fell in love with the person that you are. The not-so-flat tummy and flabby butt was just a bonus!"

"Look at me dear," he resumed all seriousness. "The moment I married you, I've had the mental preparation to see your ex-husband's image on our son's face every day. But because I love you, I've grown to love him as my own. Don't ever doubt that, please..."

Well, life manifests its miracles in mysterious ways. In her case, a Pa Pa for Junior took a longer route to appear before them. Then again, aren't the best things in life saved for the last, and to last?

CULTURE CLUB

25

CABIN CREW CULTURE

Ever caught sight of a set of cabin crew springing off their cushy seats in the waiting lounge the moment the trio of tech crew (airline lingo for cockpit crew) appears in the near distance? Ever wonder why they seem more eager to shake the skipper's hands than that of a celebrity? And why do these charming hosts sing 'Thank you for the flight' to each and every one of their colleagues after each flight?

What if it was a terrible one? Do we still flash those pearlies and join in the chorus? Absolutely. Welcome to the orientation of cabin crew culture.

Well, if you know anyone from the airline, you've probably heard stories of how newbies go through a phase of accelerated learning by means of our infamous in-flight boot-camp. Up in the sky, seniority rules. It is all about the colour of our uniform. What about those in the same rank? We then play the numbers game. Each one of us comes 'tagged' with a staff number; and many a times, the level of respect accorded depends on it, as it is indicative of when each flight attendant had joined the airline. The larger the staff number the more junior the steward or stewardess is. It is not uncommon to hear one whisper to another, "Eh, what's her staff number? So *yaya* (arrogant) papaya!" Don't ask me why they use 'papaya' other than it rhymes. Or "Oh… so he's XXXX number. Don't 'play play' (mess around) *ah*."

Seniority is an advantage, allowing first picks. Be it a choice of main course - from whatever that's available after passengers have had their fill, work positions (guess who gets the zone with the most empty seats), rest shift (most prefer the second shift, leaving them re-charged for the next meal service), bunk choices (make or break a good sleep. See chapter 'Are We Alone?')

Even when one enters the galley of another zone, proper acknowledgement has to be given or risk being ordered out. Likewise when you need to borrow say, an ice bucket from the other steward in galley Y, proper protocol states that permission has to be given. Sounds serious? Not really. It's all about the Ps and Qs that carry us far, anywhere we go. As service providers in a world famous international airline, the 'Thank you's and 'Sorry's roll off our tongues faster than Usain Bolt at the crack of a gun.

As I learnt very quickly in my first few months, the 'addressing-by-name' culture is serious business. Each time we encounter a colleague, be it in the galley or cabin, it had to be a polite "Excuse me so-and-so, may I…" Only the higher ranks can get away with generic terms like 'dear', 'handsome' or *'sayang'* (dear).

Junior stewards conduct headcounts before the coach leaves for the hotel or airport and double up as porters during the absence of one at certain stations. Meanwhile junior stewardesses are in charge of collecting tips for the bus driver from other crew members. Once checked into the hotel, the set of crew would wait for their room keys to be distributed by, who else? The juniors. If the signatures are required, the supervisor would be the first, followed by the rest.

In a nutshell, being at the bottom of the hierarchy, choices are pretty much equivalent to naught.

Boot-camp, as the name suggests, is helmed by seniors who will not bat an eyelid before chewing a newbie's head off, should any of them screw up. And fumble they probably will during the initial months or even years for the incorrigible ones in a perpetual dreamland state.

Our term for it? Zap. If you *kena* zapped, it simply means that you have been corrected in a less-than-forgiving manner. The usual reaction would be one of fear followed by more fumbling. Well, at least that was what happened to me during those unforgettable flights. Many tears were shed in the privacy of the lavatory as I did not want them to have the pleasure of laughing at my snotty red nose.

That said, not all are done in malice. In fact, most well-meaning seniors give constructive criticism. Though, some could improve on their communication skills. I've had my fair share of being hollered at across the aisle, much to the alarm of passengers. During full flights where time is of essence, seniors have absolutely no extra minutes to gently hold the juniors by the hand. If you expect them to go through the load of mistakes with the patience of Sister Maria in *The Sound of Music*...

Dream on.

More often than not, the seniors are the ones setting the overall mood for the flight and responsible for motivating the entire set. The list of names for each flight could be accessed through our cabin crew website. It is this very list that decides whether some would report dutifully for work or call in sick in mysteriously high numbers. Others who fear tainting a clean medical record would drag their feet to the airport with a heavy heart.

It's the set of crew who makes or breaks the flight, not the passengers.

While the culture may seem daunting to some, exploiting even, but we all agree that it has made the majority of us better workers. A few meek ones crumble, fumble and tumble out of the job altogether. New flight attendants who can survive the first year are usually good to fly. I must admit that the initial months were tough. Those who could not adapt would try all means to break the bond of fifteen months, without paying the penalty of a four figure sum. Pampered individuals from well-to-do families empty their wallets readily while the rest cried their way through apprenticeship. The funny thing is, once you've gone through months of job pressure, you naturally spring a defence mechanism. Gradually, it doesn't seem all doom and gloom after all.

I remember dreading to leave for the airport during the first few months of flying. My folks used to drive me to work and each time we drew closer to the control tower, my stomach would ritually begin a complex session of Chinese-knots tying. The churning would follow. Seeing my cold fingers clenching my tummy, Mum would sigh and asked if I really wanted to go through the ordeal.

I am mighty relieved those days are behind me now. When I joined at the raw age of twenty-one, the senior crew had plenty of stories to share. I was given the impression that while they worked hard, they played just as hard, if not more. Those were the days when rock hard ice cream (not thawed on time) and charred bread rolls were thrown at the junior attendant responsible for them. He or she later had to explain and apologize to each and every passenger for the service lapse. They learn fast then, really fast.

Over time, some aspects of crew culture have eroded. The younger generation has certainly become more vocal and articulate in their thoughts. Thirteen years ago, it was almost unheard of to hear a junior talk back to a senior attendant or supervisor. These days, the crew-in-charge would be lucky to get a decent, warm main course waiting in the warming cabinet while the rest tuck in. Dispensing my two cents' worth took certain tact as well. Overdo it and the younger crew would deem me a nag.

Well, but one thing's for sure. The respect that one demands from a mere colour code or staff number exists no more. You want respect? You jolly well earn it.

26

SURVIVAL OF THE FITTEST

When I was promoted after four and a half years, it was through what we called "auto promo". If one's disciplinary and medical record was clean and the fleet needed an expansion in crew numbers, one would automatically expect a congratulatory letter and a subsequent visit to the tailor. And most definitely, an excuse for a new shade of eye shadow to match the new uniform.

Shortly after my promotion, the management decided that auto promo lacked excitement, the mental challenge and the proverbial carrot to dangle in front of its employees. A change of system was in place. The name of the game? Survival of the fittest. Not surprisingly, the rest said aye and the rest is history.

With stakes raised, the cabin crew sat up. They could no longer rest on their laurels and expect someone to push their butt up the career ladder just by 'doing time'. The rules had been re-written. Players with the highest overall scores win the right to don new coloured uniforms. The crew community was set abuzz again, peppered with the occasional over-enthusiastic appreciation of this 'clever' idea, neatly summarized in four-letter words.

Crew circulars were snapped up and many pored over latest

details of the new system. Record took a percentage portion, ward leader's review and recommendation another, while check appraisals, passenger comments, ECA (extra curricular activities) and a written test on product knowledge made up the rest. Make the cut and you'll be eligible for the interview round, helmed by a panel of three from management. It seemed a move in the right direction to get the crew motivated. With the majority jumping on the study wagon and improving on the overall performance, what can be wrong about this change?

Check appraisals by a senior colleague are conducted onboard on a one-to-one basis, somewhat like a mystery shopper who springs a last minute review on the unsuspecting crew. It serves its secondary purpose of keeping us on tenterhooks, and on our best at all times. We could be on our best alright, but is the appraiser, mood wise? At times, we get disappointing appraisals from overly expectant leaders with varying standards. One lousy check is enough to drag the average down, wiping out all past efforts to maintain high scores of at least eighty percent. While there is a column for the one being appraised to acknowledge the non/acceptance of the lackluster check report, how many of us have the guts to do so, much less in front of the appraiser?

Suddenly, the office was swarmed with eager members yearning to shake their ward leader's hands, to make themselves 'known'. A very necessary gesture to stand out among the sea of what we call, 'shrimps'. Some even kept a printout of leaders' profiles and set that to memory, rattling off their names when paths are crossed in the office. To the latter, we are but a staff number. Making recommendations on which pretty staff number to promote would be a case of 'Eeny, meeny, miny moe'. I refused to do so when I was eligible for the promotion exercise. This act of utter hypocrisy was too much to shake on.

Others sacrifice precious days off giving training classes while the missus and kids grumble that daddy's never home. And we are not talking about ten or twenty lessons, but a minimum of a year's worth in order to even stand a chance of being a little red dot among the continents. The last I checked, the queue to be a trainer stretched far and wide.

Onboard, they flexed their facial muscles and up the charms on the passengers in a bid to reap complimentary letters. Suddenly, a mountain of letters flooded the office, hitting an all time high ratio of compliments versus complaints. Some passengers voiced their displeasure at overzealous crew who kept pushing comment forms into their hands, asking for "feedback so we can improve." It proved far more successful than the courtesy campaign! The department lady did her bit of complaining when she struggled to find her desk amid the pile, and soon, they decided to shelf it altogether as an appraisal requirement.

Others did a different form of flexing. Colleagues became wary of one another. Anyone could be a potential threat to his or her promotion chances. Thus, a flurry of letters came in, only this time it was targeted at fellow colleagues for petty service lapses that could easily be resolved onboard. This form of writing each other in, raised temperatures and soured relations, not to mention increase the workload of those handling these paper back-stabs. I recall this incident where a senior steward reported another to the Singapore Customs just as he made his way past.

"The stewardess behind has something that may interest you," was all he said. She did, as the girl had pocketed a new design of the airline's poker cards with the intention of adding it to her collection. No matter how small the item, it is considered pilferage. In the eyes of every company, a big no-no.

Certain ECAs awarded points crucial to meet the final cut-off mark. Despite fatigue or plain disinterest, crew members participated in several activities in order to spruce up their curriculum vitae. Some turned to drama where the arts group has successfully churned out singers and actors who are now active in the media industry. Others participated in tennis, golf or whatever the senior management was dabbling in at the moment. What better way to draw a big highlight across one's face than attempt eighteen holes with the management? It was not a waste of time for some, who later fell in love with their new hobbies and stayed on, promotion or not. Good for them.

Unfortunately, it has also brought out the ugly side of us. The sudden increase in volunteers for the charity homes under our care prompted all to question the agenda behind our motives. The rush to be in photos which are splashed across in-house magazines confirm their dubious intentions. Whenever senior management would be present for a special celebratory event with the old folks, guess who are the ones to turn up? The very same ones found in every picture, standing next to a Vice-President or some worthy senior manager. On a brighter note, the thin silver lining about this entire charade brought about a heightened awareness on the airline's adopted charities.

A senior stewardess preferring to work behind the scenes, set up her own charity group of 'angels', with the mission of bringing joy to the less fortunate in both Indonesia and Singapore. These 'angels' often fly off to Indonesia with food and gifts for potentially wayward kids. They earned no ECA points nor 'fame', only reciprocal love of the kids and true camaraderie of like-minded souls. Bro befriended a few 'angels' and shortly, became a convert.

M.C. rates are the lowest at this time of the year. Not that it reflects the truth about the crew's health of course. Those who are caught by bouts of flu struggle to work in order to earn those important extra points. A team mate who was next to collapsing begged his doctor for a steroid shot to get through the flight. Silly? When you learn that you missed the mark by a mere point due to a miserable sick leave, maybe it doesn't seem that insane after all.

From the time the promotion exercise is announced, all will set on a feverish study of past years circulars (usually untouched prior to this change), each rich with vital information ranging from service procedures, food preparation and practically anything under the sky. The problem with reading through thick stacks of circulars is that one could easily be confused with preceding or superseding updates or training materials. Aircraft changes, new in-flight procedures and menus often had us flipping to and fro the pages to confirm the latest. Over the years, some diligent colleagues came up with their version of the 'ten-year series' - a popular compilation of past test questions and answers students are familiar with.

In order to beef up the already bulging compilation, some go to the extent of loitering around rooms where tests on product knowledge are conducted. Hoping to chance upon familiar faces (or not, if one has a skin of a rhino,) whom they pounce on them like old friends and try to weasel a question or two from the tight-lipped candidates. It was everyone for him or herself. The management would advise those taking the tests - leak out any information and your friend scores, not you. Your friend goes through to interview round, not you. Your friend gets promoted, not you.

Ok, point taken.

Not by all actually. Some of us believe in strength in numbers, gathering a few trustworthy colleagues, forming our own study groups. This method has tremendous results, provided that no one holds back on sharing.

So let's say the first hurdle has been crossed and you go through the holy gates of the interview room. No matter how much preparation has gone into this deciding moment of truth, many fall victim to the jitters when facing the panel. Not one has emerged without sweaty palms. How does one prove him or herself within a short fifteen minutes? Can one really impress the heck out of weary interviewers who have heard every brilliant answer imaginable?

A conspiracy theory made its rounds. The candidates are already pre-selected, they say. The interview round is only for formality sake. Some speculate that the pictures of selected ones come with a bold red tick across their fact sheets and the rest, a definitive cross. In my opinion, if one doesn't possess the bare leadership essentials, the company would never take the risk of ticking his or her picture because all it takes is one rotten apple of a leader to contaminate the whole crate.

The image of the airline is kept youthful, thus the need for the crew to remain as such. A steward approaching the big four was attempting his third shot at the senior position. The skinny man decided to up his chances by seeking the help of the good doctor who happens to be a favourite among celebrities and the crew alike. "Make me young," he asked. And a couple of Botox injections into the lined forehead and corners of his prematurely wrinkled eyes later, the rejuvenated man went in with a new face of confidence.

And yes, he got it this time. Maybe it was the shots that helped, maybe he was just third time lucky.

The list of successful candidates is announced via the crew website, receiving more visits than the top porn website. Everyone reads with bated breath, slapping their thighs in joy when the deserving are finally recognized or/and shouting expletives when bootlickers succeed in pulling the wool over the panel's eyes. It is inevitable that some would sleep a happy man or woman that night, knowing the past months or years of effort have paid off while others are left dejected and demoralized.

More often than not, just doing one's best may not suffice. A girlfriend laments the absence of her name on the recent list, yet again, for the fourth time. Eleven years, she says. Is that fair? Do we reward the hardworking man or woman who quietly does more than his or her fair share or the scheming individual who takes the shortcut to more effective ends?

The system isn't perfect, then again, which appraisal system is? As with every organisation, only the fittest survives the corporate jungle. While not all end up getting the coveted promotion, at least the benefits are reaped in some shape or form. All that studying minimizes the awkward "Er, please wait a moment while I check it out," to enquiring passengers. The preparation for the interview makes us more confident service providers. As far as I'm concerned, every dog would have its day. Maybe it takes a longer time but it will, someday, somehow.

27

COCKPIT VS CABIN

I witnessed the beauty of Singapore's nightlights as the aircraft descended onto the runway at Changi Airport. Not by the side window of the crew seat, but a spectacular full frontal view from the cockpit. I was a trainee then and was hesitant. It was a one-off invitation by the affable Indian captain who simply remarked, "If not now, then when?" I am glad I took his offer. That was the one and only time I experienced the panty-wetting thrill and adrenaline rush of a plane landing as the surrounding lights swooshed by in a bright blur.

In the span of my career, I've had the pleasure of flying with this captain on two more occasions, each with a favourable impression of the heavyset man with an infectious thunder-loud laughter and absolutely zero airs. I tend to remember the few pilots under the cabin crew's classification of - 'very nice', 'irritating' and plain 'cocky'. The rest are those whom we have very little contact with, meaning that they neither took much interest in us nor irritate. The general impression the public has of the airline family is that of, well, a family. As with everything in life, nothing is picture perfect except airbrushed pin-ups.

Some of us want nothing to do with the tech crew. There has always been a divide between the two.

The cabin crew serves the cockpit before or more typically, after the passengers. The girls would be the ones knocking on the door. "Two or three men facing each other for the past few hours, a pretty face would be a welcome change to break the monotony," a supervisor once remarked. It is of certain truth as experience has shown. Most pilots are so delighted by the sight of a fresh young girl that they would try to hold them back with lengthy conversation. I say this not on a negative note. Most of them are just friendly colleagues bored to tears and seeking an outlet to fill a bucket of spit. Indeed, some can yak until the cows come home. The more interesting conversationalists even make one forget that the cabin awaits.

Most crew-in-charge prefer to serve the cockpit after the cabin's been settled, but if time permits, we would try to oblige. The problem lies with the few who choose to catch us in the midst of service and expect to be served immediately. The call would come smack in the middle of our circus act of juggling drinks, table set-ups, heating meals, toilet checks and whatnots. Which brings to question : through the CCTV, can't they see how busy we are?

The tech crew usually have their choice of main course from the First or Business class menu, after the passengers have eaten. While they are limited to the main course and fruit basket, a few are not shy to request the additional lobster bisque or scoop of caviar. It usually depends on how nicely they put the request across, the availability of their requests and the mood of the cabin crew. After all, we are colleagues. You just have to say your 'please' and thank you'.

Demanding tech crew + easy-going cabin crew = Our response would typically be, "Never mind. They want, we try to give."

Demanding + intolerant = "Tell them that the paxs ate up everything."

Nice + easy-going = "Recommend the pistachio crème brulee from First Class to the tech crew, since the captain is so nice."

Nice + intolerant = "Okay, bring these up if there's leftover. No time? No need then."

One thing that irks the cabin crew is that most pilots seem reluctant to pull their rears off the seat. They are served an individual tray, which is consumed off the lap and in the tight confinement of the cockpit. We usually wait for a half hour or a call from the flight deck for the retrieval of trays. A rare few will clear their own trays. Sadly, the majority takes on the typical food-court mentality of expecting the cleaner to do so. Even when they leave for a toilet break after a meal, their trays remain in the cockpit. What's so difficult about taking out your own tray, I wonder. Is it the so-called rank divide that renders the self-clearance of trays and cups beneath you?

I used to hate it when they pop out asking for 'difficult' drinks that took more than a squeeze of a carton or a pull of a bottle cap. Sometimes it would be honey lemon, iced Milo or even iced mocha. If that is not bad enough, some choose to linger in the galley while I fix the drink. I never got over the discomfort of having someone stare at my back. It is fine to come up with odd requests during the sleep-inducing lull periods, but not during peak hours when I was already saddled with countless cabin orders. I would spurt a curt but restrained "Please wait" instead of a more truthful "Can't you see I'm busy, damn it?!"

But of course, we get really considerate ones who not only wait for an appropriate time to make their requests, they attempt to help themselves to the drinks in the chiller. They take the effort to note the carts for the tray stowage and quietly relieve the crew of this before slipping back into the cockpit.

A particularly outstanding colleague gets my vote. The Kolkata-born captain does much more than fly the skies. He gets down and dirty on his knees to pilot hygiene projects in impoverished villages of India, helping the destitute with medical and childcare needs. He does it not on a whim of fancy, but has been trudging ahead on this path of love and giving for the past five years.

What a sterling example of a selfless man who made good in his career and does not hesitate to give back to society. The best set of blueprints for his two boys.

Once outstationed, the tech and cabin crew do not mingle. Part of the reason stems from different hotel locations, with the tech crew often putting up in centrally located ones. They have a strong union to thank for. Another reason is due to the fact that both sides never really gelled as a family but only as colleagues; the indifferent behavior and a chasm in pay packages between both crews could be a factor. Thus, you could hardly blame some of the animosity aimed at the few captains who throw their weight around indiscriminately.

There was a 747 captain who gave the cabin crew in the upper deck a hard time with endless demands, all at wrong timings. The complex leader hit boiling point. When the flight came to a close, the captain had the cheek to ask for a bottle of liquor to be 'signed off'. "Sure Captain, I'll just have to document this. Please countersign the report afterwards," he calmly told the man when he came into the galley with a bag ready to bag his bottle. The captain glared at him in disbelief but said nothing before taking wide, thumping steps back to the cockpit. A well deserved mini-triumph.

That said, many single stewardesses wouldn't mind a beau in a nice, five figure-earning second officer or captain. There is a Chinese saying : 近水楼台先得月 - the closer one is, to their desired goal or object, the better his or her chances are of getting it. If one's goal is to attain a beau in the form of a pilot, being a stewardess will bring her one step closer. I'm sure the reverse holds true, evident in the high number of marriages between the two groups. 'Mission' accomplished, many girls eventually quit after marriage. No one wants their woman to slave onboard if his bank account can afford it.

'Tryers' among the tech crew are typically in long, tired marriages who no longer find their spouses visually enticing; especially when the latter are up against willing, young impressionable girls who take to lavish gifts with zero strings attached. Such combinations are not common and temporal as both sides graze on seemingly greener pastures. In some cases, the owner threatens castration as a warning to the wandering cattle.

Some remove their wedding bands before making a move, not knowing that the lighter tell-tale shade on the finger says it all. Others blatantly disregard their ornaments completely (as well as that on the target's finger), earning themselves a filthy name in the airline and little respect.

On the reverse, we find the occasional scenario where girl meets married boy and throws herself at him. Some will cushion her fall and return all dignity to its rightful owner by a subtle hint of his married status. Others delight in the sudden windfall and lap it all up.

A few choked, a few gloated but the majority return home to their family with a clean conscience and story to share.

28

THOU SHALL NOT STEAL

I was dining in an Indian restaurant in Gloucester, London when my ears pricked at a conversation between the owner and a patron. The latter introduced himself as a steward of a particular Asian airline (not ours, thankfully) and wondered if he was interested in the quality tins of Ossetia caviar he had on hand. Both spoke in hushed tones but my ears have this innate ability to pick up juicy bits of information. Obviously, the steward had pilfered from the aircraft. The owner was interested in his wares, though not the obscenely expensive salted fish roes. He was willing to pay for smokes, i.e. duty-free cigarettes from the airport each time he flew to London. Moments later, they had a done deal. The agreed price was two and a half times that of the duty-free version; twice of those retailed in London. It was a win-win.

Sure, if you can chew more than you have bitten off. A steward certainly choked when he landed in a particular station and was caught with sixteen cartons of the nicotine sticks in his otherwise half empty cargo bag. He went down in airline history. The moment he was sent back to base, he was made history alright.

A girlfriend from XX airline was unhappy about a recent

downgrade of accommodation. They used to stay in this excellent service apartment in Auckland. In fact, it remains the best she has experienced as a stewardess. The self-contained room was a home away from home, with a kitchen so well equipped that it rivaled any home- proud owner. Toaster, pots and pans, carving knives, sauce boats, cheese graters, blenders, oven - you name it, they had it. The crew marveled at the laundry dryer sitting pretty next to the washer, complete with a choice of liquid detergent or powder. The array of branded toiletries was impressive, to say the least. Finally! A station where they could leave with fresh-smelling clothes; great for the next flight.

Unfortunately, some had planned to leave with more than clean clothes. Shortly after they started the lease, the hotel management complained to the company that items were pilfered from the rooms. The alleged theft could not be verified due to the high turnover. It was a case of one party's words against the other. The hotel staff decided to take matters into their own hands after consulting the airline. Prior to checkout, a set of crew was asked to gather in a room where a bag search was conducted with their approval. Five out of the eighteen bags produced a souvenir. Soft, fluffy towels and bathrobes were the common loot, but check this out. One junior stewardess managed to pack a frying pan into her cabin luggage. Another loved the toaster so much that she intended to borrow it. For good.

I guess it was fair that they received the boot from the hotel. Not wanting to rub salt into her wounds, I kept my opinion to myself though. It doesn't make economic nor commercial sense to lose dollars replacing items that catches the crew's fancy. The rest of the law-abiding lot cried foul. The few black sheep had tainted the name of the airline and cut short their stay at this wonderful service apartment. They were thrown out like rowdy drunks from the pub.

And get this. I have heard of a steward from another airline who proudly displays a piece of quality carpet in his living room. The cunning fella had relieved the chambermaid of her duty to vacuum it. He had basically cut it out from under a bed in one of the hotels. I was disgusted when I heard this. Taking little items for memory sake like the room stationery or mini bottles of bath gel is acceptable, but to cut out an entire piece of carpet was a totally different ball game.

A flight attendant from a well-known European airline was caught with several bottles of champagne pilfered off the aircraft. It was rumoured that he was tempted by the many earlier successful transactions he had made with a local buyer. It was good money. Easy too. Or so he thought. He was the kid who couldn't resist the cookie jar; he was also the kid who lost his grip on the cookie jar and hurt himself real bad when it smashed to smithereens.

The Chinese have a wise saying : 上得山多终遇虎。 If you make one too many trips up the mountains, chances are, you would encounter the tiger.

With his name splashed out in the newspapers and a handsome pension forfeited; he was to pack up in shame. Well, I guess the proverbial tiger did catch up with him.

29

Sistas

A relative once remarked, "Girl ah, you better not mix with the airline boys too often. So many *buayas* (players) and *Ah Kuas* (effeminate men)." I laughed it off.

After more than a decade in the airline, I've met them all. The fatherly, the stoic, the 'zappy', the lonely, the clown, the gentleman, the tempted and last but not least, my relative's abhorred players of the love game. Most outsiders are under the wrong impression that the airline men play more than their fair share. While it is true that our setting is a lot more thrilling than the typical office environment, most stay grounded to a single notion - Hurt No One.

As for the alternatively lifestyled, there are many in the airline industry. It is no surprise as the jet-set lifestyle suits them to a tee. Gossip sessions with them are always interesting, often peppered with the exaggerated hand gestures and funny anecdotes. A similar trait is their meticulous attention to the smallest detail, from making the prettiest dessert presentation, frothiest cappuccino to the neatest galley setup. In fact, most of my makeup tips came from an ex-team boy, Raymond whom we affectionately call "Ramona". He was the one who introduced me to a well-kept secret of drinking

South African Rooibus tea when I lamented about the drying effects of the cabin air.

A friend of Ling attempted suicide four years ago. The man D, was thrown in depression after his live-in lover of fifteen years left him for another. We were shocked to hear the news as the couple had been very close. D was wanton in his spending habits, often draining his account on big labels for his boyfriend, whom he affectionately called 'My Pooh Bear'. He thought the world of him and planned to get married in Amsterdam. It was later rumoured that Pooh Bear met a wealthy Swedish guy who swept him off his paws. While choosing one's path to happiness is a personal decision, we still empathized with D. But what little help could we offer? Already in his fifties, he had given his youth to Pooh and wanted no other. Shortly, he retired from the airline and we lost contact with him completely.

There was a good-looking steward from an earlier team who boasts of a partner in every port. The usual laments I heard from him were about the lack of time to rest because he had to juggle the many activities with his boyfriends. Why not settle for the one you really like spending quality time with, I queried. The tall, slim-built man cupped his sharp chin with both hands and explained that he fought hard not to take more than one dish at the smorgasbord but lost.

Okay, I reasoned with him. Don't go for the smorgasbord in the first place. There is only so much one could stomach. Stick to the menu of a brilliant chef who could please your sensory buds from the appetizers to desserts. And choose one who rotates the dishes in case you get bored easily.

He agreed with me. "Can't change overnight though," he said. The last time I checked, the man confessed to a poor excessive diet still. Though a more discerning choice of ala-carte buffet.

I remember this particular senior steward. The olive-skinned, moustached funnyman was a favourite among the crew, often leaving them in stitches. He made no effort to conceal his preference for all things male and French. When we operated a flight to Paris together a few years ago, our conversation strayed to the topic of pleasuring men. The girls listened intently, ears pricked as the grand master of erotica, as he so proclaimed himself to be, gave us a lesson on stimulating the senses. We giggled in hushed tones as we stood huddled in the galley, trying to overcome the bashfulness while not wanting to miss out on vital tips.

Exasperated, the man pouted his lips in disapproval and asked the group, "Hey, do you girls understand or not?" With his arms held akimbo, he looked around the galley, chanced upon the fruit basket and fished out a Del Monte. "Ok, that was theory. Now for the practical," he proposed, shoving the yellow prop towards us.

The girls squirmed and waved their hands in refusal. The sporting man then proceeded to peel the skin off, shape the tip of the banana with a clever saw of his teeth and gave us the most disgusting demonstration one could ever do with a piece of fruit.

I could never look at a banana the same way again.

SAYONARA

30

So You Wanna Fly
The Skies Huh?

The three Bs encapsulate the essence of our finer flight attendants – Beauty, Brawn and Brains.

As I trawl the online forums, one common topic stands out – the entry requirement to be a cabin crew. Most concerns are centered on appearances. Questions regarding facial blemishes, body art, skin colour, even freckles are debated furiously. A few are anxious to know if their tattoos mean an instant exit. One was even prepared to laser away the inked barbs circling his arm. Others asked for tips on skin whitening. Anyone who stumbles onto the website would probably think it is a beauty forum.

It goes without saying, any frontline personnel should be pleasant in appearance; however, you need not be Miss Universe material. Having clear skin helps. Let's face it, being served by a pimply attendant with dirty nails and foul breath isn't the most appetising before a meal. There are zero issues with skin tone or colour, evident in the multi-racial members in our airline family.

In my humble opinion, what is most important and what

separates the average stewardess or steward from the really good ones, is the beauty within. A cliché it might be, but here's what it really means :

Attitude – If you think good service is only about food and drinks, passengers are better off with a self-help counter or vending machine. Service does not draw a line between customer and service provider. It requires not subservience, but a genuine interest in putting the comfort of your guests on top priority, even if it means going out of your way to do so. Our crew goes the extra mile not because they have to, but because they want to. Ask yourself - when it comes to the crunch, is it them or me first?

Grace – it is always easier to mirror niceness. It takes a tougher cookie not to waver in the face of disregard and outright disrespect.

Humanness – Empathy is the invisible thread that links us. Having a good EQ (emotional intelligence quotient) helps too. Do you have the innate ability to understand the unspoken? Do you feel the urge to reach out or address those needs?

Tenacity – Do you make lemonade out of lemons that life throws you? Do you stare at a wall blocking your way, defeated, or do you find a way to flank that wall? It takes a mental fortitude to brave challenges even when shortcuts beckon.

In summary, the human heart prompts small acts of kindness which is re-enacted on every flight. And none of which takes a chunk off our backs. While it is easy to pretend not to see avenues for the extra mile, the fact is, feigned ignorance plays down hard on your conscience. That is, if you have a conscience to begin with.

If you possess the above, welcome to the family. Let me give you the low-down on what to expect.

Brawn is certainly needed in our line of work. I'm not referring to rippling muscles per se but physical stamina and endurance. The mad rush of duties on every flight slowly catches up on us.

For instance, a Hong Kong turnaround is equivalent to a seven hours 'workout'. After a couple of years, wear and tear sets in. Glucosamine tops the list of drugstore purchases on US trips. For the elderly parents? Sadly no, it's damage control for our own aching knees. Worn down by irregular meals and jetlag affected sleep, it isn't surprising to find one's energy levels dipping in later years.

Brains, the grey matter. While a degree is not part of entry requirements, content between your ears is still imperative. Being worldly-wise helps you PR with passengers beyond brainless topics like the weather and shopping lists. Upload news-worthy materials to your mental chip and impress the sockettes off our well-heeled travellers. Smile after giving your two cents worth on world matters and watch them do a double take.

Being well-travelled ambassadors, many approach us for travel tips. Who best to advise on stations that feature the best shopping, yummy eats, scenic sights and festive celebrations? While it is true that some colleagues choose to remain holed up to hibernate and recuperate in the hotel room during layovers, others bitten by the travel bug venture far and wide in search of exciting sites and sights.

Here's an upside of being a stewardess. If not for this job, I wouldn't have the money nor opportunities to imprint my footsteps in places where I had the time of my life :

- Riding gentle albeit smelly camels amid the majestic and ancient pyramids of Cairo
- Shouting at the top of my lungs atop the Statue of Liberty, after a slice of to-die-for Oreo cheesecake from The Cheesecake Factory, New York
- Slurping piping hot clam chowder in bread bowls to warm the soul while 'behind bars' on the Rock (Alcatraz, San Francisco)

- Picnicking on a lazy afternoon with freshly baked baguettes, French butter and escargots from the nearby supermarket, under the magnificent Eiffel Tower
- Feeding plump grey squirrels with cashews amid lush flora and fauna in London's Hyde Park
- Immersing myself in the cotton clouds on Table Mountain, Cape Town
- An overnight karaoke session that climaxed with a breathtaking view of the sun rising over Hong Kong's Victoria's Peak
- Chasing (shouldn't have, but I was so excited to see them!) cute penguins on Penguin Island, Adelaide (after a two-hour drive!)
- Snapping at the devil (ok, snapping pictures of the Tasmanian Devil)
- Snowball fighting on pristine Mount Titlis, Zurich
- Trying hard not to stare at the pleasure girls behind glass windows in Amsterdam
- Dining onboard a classy restaurant-cum-boat while stealing moves from the belly-dancers along the River Nile
- And the list goes on …

Lastly, a word of caution. Brace yourself for an adult world where the sudden earning power, lease of freedom, peer pressure, ease of booze and smokes can render the tame wild. It is like throwing a kid into *Willy Wonka's Chocolate Factory* with the strict instruction not to binge him or herself silly.

Some turn materialistic, splurging most part of the monthly salary on stuff they do not need. The sixth LV bag because it is cheaper in Paris, the blue Rolex Oyster that everyone is raving about, a Coach keychain to match the wallet at a sale. An ex-colleague still maintains a deficit in his bank account after fifteen years of flying, while another maxed out three credit cards with no immediate means to pay.

This is a job where parents and spouses will have a hard time keeping tabs on you. Time difference, street roaming after meals and the frequent gathering in crew rooms let you dictate the time to be contactable. Sounds excellent? Those with a deviant agenda on their minds would certainly say aye – with wild late night partying and womanising on their cards. Stories of airline girls who moonlight in Hong Kong and oil-rich Saudi states remain to be proven.

To the homely type, are you prepared for days away from home and loved ones? Do you mind that the family dog barks, failing to recognize you after a nine-day trip? Or that you might miss the poignant milestones in your baby's growth? Or can't be without mum's cooking for more than a day?

Clearly, the cabin crew environment is not like any other. Do you have what it takes to be one? Compare my notes against a personal checklist and you decide.

31

Hello & Goodbye

When I hit the end of my first year and dad didn't bring the subject up, I tried my luck for the second year. Before I could say 'quit', the certificate of appreciation I had received some time later screamed ten years. A decade!

Why did I choose to leave after thirteen years? I didn't. Not in spirit anyway. The physical departure involved a personal decision to embark on another journey in my life. It is one which I trod precariously at first.

It started out as just another flight to Frankfurt. Being the senior personnel in the economy zone, I was boarding passengers at door two. After the umpteenth passenger, the perfunctory greetings and checking of passes became mundane, to say the least. Then He came along. A lock of eyes and a most beautiful smile was all it took to take my facial muscles to a major stretch, only this time, the reason to smile was personal.

Don't get me wrong. Not every cute, brown-eyed hunk that comes my way renders me weak in the knees. He did and still does. We had a history which dates back to 2002 when the mutual attraction was hampered by a major roadblock, the Girlfriend.

Nothing transpired and I exited from the picture with a new-found respect for the guy. Life went on and we never heard from each other since.

During the twelve-hour flight, I sneaked peeks at him in a deep slumber, oblivious to the world. I later learnt from one of my team girls, that he had fallen asleep while waiting for a request of aspirin that never came. Not wanting to bother the crew, he bore with the discomfort of a headache and attempted to sleep it off. The flight was full and demanding as expected. By the time the passengers streamed past me during disembarkation, I was ready to crash. He loitered around and slowly walked towards me with a smile. My hand instinctively went to tame stray hairs on my French twist while licking my lips to make them glisten. Darn it, why didn't I slap on the gloss before landing?

The smile never left his face. He slipped me a name card and I acted cool. Sure, let's keep in touch, I said. With that, He left me nursing a drumming heart and burning blush.

For a month, I wore the name card raw, retrieving it from the safe haven of my wallet and placing it back after a close study of his every detail, each time plumping up the guts to dial the number I had long memorised at the back of my hand. Why did he give it to me? Why did he stay back just to talk to me? Am I imagining things? Maybe he is now regretting not asking for my number. Maybe it's simply a casual gesture people do all the time with acquaintances. Maybe he was the last few to disembark because his seat at 62C was at the rear to begin with.

Oh, what was I thinking of? Just pick up the darn phone and call him on the pretext of some important matter which would sound incredulously lame. I'll most definitely make a fool of myself and he'd thank his lucky stars that the sparks that ignited years back fizzled like a can of day-old coke.

"Aiyah girl, why worry so much? At least give it a shot." My mentor and friend Ling urged me to cast my unfounded doubts aside. She is a go-getter. Me? Well, I am shy. Besides, I never had to make the first move on a man.

"What first move? He gave you the name card. Isn't that a big hint for you to tango, you silly woman?" she chided like a big sister. "Give me his e-mail. I'll drop a greeting. That way, there are zero chances of you possibly babbling out of control."

She was right. I could write him instead. A short hello mail to a friend lost and found.

I sat in front of the PC, fingers poised over the keyboard. After a while, I realised that they had started to stiffen due to inactivity. It was more difficult than I had expected. I needed to craft something casual with a witty twist, something that catches his attention more than the common "Dear So-and-So, it was great to have met you. Blah blah blah…" But here I was, struggling with the first sentence.

Finally, I decided that a one-liner would suffice.

"Hi, it's me." Talk about short and sweet.

The reply came almost instantaneously. Before I could utter the word "mental block", we would send a flurry of e-mails to and fro, each rich with content, none of the uncomfortable virtual silence. Within a span of three months, we had gotten to know much of each other. Gradually, we got bolder as the bubbles of chemistry brewed. With each email that came, my heart soared as I ventured if this man had been sent beyond the mere purpose of increasing the list of male suitors - all had so far failed to meet the mark horribly.

Six months later, we finally decided to meet without the safety net of our monitors. "It's my birthday. Treat me to a drink," I playfully demanded. That night, I fussed over my hair and makeup. The heaps of clothes on my bed laid testament to the countless outfits I skimmed through. It is true that happiness makes a woman's skin glow like no other miracle water can. The sheer excitement of the first date radiated through the epidermis of my rosy cheeks. After taking one last satisfied glance at the mirror, I left to meet him.

The look on his face made the hour-long preening and priming well worth it, because he later described his reaction as having to scrape his lower jaw off the pavement. I stole a quick look at his casual ensemble of a fitting black tee and Levis. I was pleased. He had managed to pull it off. Ok, I admit I was checking out his tight butt. So sue me.

The sweet man brought me to an animal shelter to visit the three dogs he rescued. He had a penchant for scooping furry strays off the streets and finding homes for them. The trunk was loaded with cat and dog food, ready to quell the hunger pangs of our four-legged friends. Animal lover. Need I say more?

He then drove to a forgotten parking site. The silence of the night was interrupted only by active timbals of the cicadas' choir. There was neither a vehicle nor soul in sight. In fact, it was so dark that I'd be lucky to see beyond the windscreen. My antenna went on instant alert, as did the tiny hairs on the back of my neck. Please, please don't let him turn out to be a creep.

He rummaged through some stuff in the car boot. Ropes? Knife? Kinky cuffs? I clung to the sides of the seat in bated breath. Moments later, a rather pitchy rendition of the ubiquitous birthday song floated through the cool night air and he surprised me with a cookies and cream ice-cream cake, complete with the dry ice effect. Haagen Dazs, no less.

I half-laughed in relief. It helped that he hit one of my favourite flavours on the head. We dug in with humble plastic spoons, savouring each mouthfuls of the creamy iced confection, while the radio DJ played all the right songs.

Later that night, the glorious bottle at a wine bar worked its magic on us. We shared life stories and laughed naturally like age-old friends. All the while, I gazed into his deep brown eyes. As he returned his gentle gaze on me, I knew for certain that it was reciprocal. Either that, or he was looking at me through wine-tinted glasses.

The rest of the evening went by so quickly that I dreaded the end of it. We drove back in the wee hours of the morning totally tired out. The light in the car porch was off. My folks were probably asleep by then. The car engine purred gently as we sat in it, not wanting to break the silence. Some five minutes later, we bid each other goodnight reluctantly. It must have been the fermented grape juice working my guts, because I leaned over suddenly and planted a soft kiss on his lips before bolting out the door, my heart drumming a crazy beat.

As I lay in bed and recounted the night right down to each minuscule detail, I knew I was in love. More importantly, was he? Was I too direct? Should I have waited to make the second move? After all, a respectable lady should conform to traditional Asian values and I was pretty sure that did not encompass a lip-lock on first dates. The message alert on my cell went off and I jumped. Seconds later, I squealed in delight. The text he sent before blowing virtual goodnight kisses told me exactly what I had hoped to know. He too had fallen.

Hook, line and sinker.

As Tigger would say to the Super Sleuths in *Tigger and Pooh*, "The mystery is history."

Life has opened yet another chapter. I have found the missing piece in my jigsaw. One that I look forward to with each passing day.

Months after submitting the resignation letter, I still feel very much a stewardess, more so when I meet up with ex-colleagues for a whale of a gossip session. Crew talk, alien to outsiders, reigns in our conversation. Regular updates hold my attention as I soak them up like a sponge. Not without a splattering of mild expletives.

Even now, each time a plane soars, I would most inevitably look skywards. What flight is it? Who might the supervisor be this time? Is the load full as usual? Does the announcement suck?

Just a couple of months ago, I was on a flight to Perth. Only this time, I played the reversed role of a passenger. It felt strange being greeted at the entrance and offered to be shown the way to my seat. As I strode down the aisle, the warm familiar feeling of 'home' came rushing back.

Kid you, I do not. The scent of the air freshener that hangs faintly in the cabin beckons welcomingly. The very same whiff I used to dislike and associate with lavatory clean-ups. I sensed the same adrenaline rush I used to get when the passengers started boarding. "Time to rock and roll, people," I used to say after a quick sip and visit to the lavatory. Goodness knows when will be the next opportunity we get to do that.

After some twenty minutes in my seat, I started to fidget. I wanted a feel of the compartment doors. I craved the touch of the chilling bin where I had been icing my wines and beers for the past thirteen years. I longed to take up position at the crew seat again, the very seat that provided great relief to hear "Cabin crew, to your landing stations please". I longed to cradle the silver serving tray that had seen countless of drink orders pass through it. The very tray I often swore to knock out irritating passengers with.

Working in an environment where people from all walks of life are confined in a metal tube for long hours, trying not to tear one another's hair out, has certainly stretched my limit and beyond. I developed a tolerance for nonsense I never knew I had.

That said, the majority of passengers are regular folks like us. Most understand and empathize when the workload stretches our grins inversely. I know a regular traveler who clears his own tray and drinks by taking them directly to the galley. The guy waits till the mayhem of the meal service ceases before he make his way to the galley with a box of local treats. Sounds too good to be true? Well, he is not alone. Over the years, we have had boxes of chocolates, Krispy Kremes, Polar curry puffs, Japanese cream puffs from generous, appreciative people who view the cabin crew not just as people employed to serve, but as thinking individuals who take pride in their work.

Indeed, after a good thirteen years with the airline, as I delve into the various chapters, the path down memory lane proved dearer to me than I had imagined. What started out as a biography has evolved into an insight to the world of the airline crew. What started as a clumsy newbie has matured into a seasoned senior stewardess.

My uniform hangs in the closet, not unlike a newly-wed's wedding dress. I don't intend to frame it up though. Who knows when the day would come when a whim of fancy strikes me? I might just pull it out of its resting place and relive those soaring days once more.

If I could manage to pull the zipper up, that is.

FAAQ : Frequently Asked Airline Questions

Any burning questions from the floor? Things that you've always wanted to ask but never did? Well fire away! Check out my website : www.milehiclub.sg , where my cabin crew friends and I will try to answer as many as we can.

In the meantime, here's an assortment of questions collected from internet postings and personal contributions.

1. **How much do flight attendants earn? I understand that it varies depending on the hours flown? Do you get a basic salary?**

Asking about our pay is almost equivalent to queries on a woman's age - most of us are fiercely private about our actual salary, as comparisons (and bitching) of rosters are rife. All I can reveal is that the range can be anything from $3500 – $7000 for a steward or stewardess.

You do the math : Basic salary + Station allowance + In-flight allowance = Dough for the month

Here's a rough gauge. Basic salary ranges from $900 to $2500 (depending on entry qualification and years of service).

Station allowances are fixed amounts depending on the location and number of days spent.

In-flight allowances are calculated on an hourly basis. Long-haul flights could carry a loading of 2-3 times the hourly rate.

Throw in attractive station allowances, especially on US and Europe runs and you know why long haul flights are so hot.

In fairness, the crew is allotted a balance of both long and short haul flights.

2. **Are there long-term side effects from working too long in the aircraft? I have heard rumours about stewards not being able to father sons and that one would develop health problems later in life?**

Where did you hear that ridiculous rumour from?! I know of many flight attendants with healthy babies - both boys and girls.

Personally, there are three unwelcome effects I can conclude after years of cabin confinement- major dehydration, hair loss and body aches. Dehydration is the number one enemy for our skin, creating fine lines that are way too premature. Imagine being in an air-conditioned room with the fan blowing at your face non-stop. That is how drying the cabin environment feels, so for the sake of your skin, drink up to plump up.

My girlfriends resort to snipping their tresses short after the clumps of fallen hair refused to abate despite religious application of hair tonic. This damage to our scalp is due to long hours of tying and abrasion from hair pins. Tons of hairspray to create that immaculate look doesn't alleviate the problem as well. Then again, this is the same occupational hazard as models and TV artistes.

In my opinion, our uniform is best complemented by a French twist or bun. Thus even though my scalp protested after each flight, I insisted on wearing my hair long.

As for the aches, imagine doing non-stop squats and shuttle runs almost every other day and you'll get the idea.

3. **Can a stewardess still fly if she is pregnant? What happens next?**

Pregnant stewardesses are advised to cease flying duties immediately, in view of their and the baby's safety. There is the option to convert to ground crew duties for the period of the pregnancy. However, most girls would typically keep mum for at least a month to maximize their income.

Two years ago, a junior stewardess realised that her three-month-old bulge was hardly more than a slight bump on her skinny frame. She decided to take her chances and pushed for another month of work. Another month, another sum, she figured. Another sum it was, when she overexerted herself while maneuvering the meal carts. The hospital bills did amount to quite a bit after she lost her baby and spent two months of unpaid leave nursing a broken heart. How do you put a figure on tears and the loss of an unborn child?

Another stewardess had an 'ingenious' plan to keep her baby under wraps - lose five to eight kilos before she gets pregnant. So that, by the time she is two months pregnant, the uniform would have filled up nicely. Theoretically, that sounded feasible, but the last time I saw her, I could have sworn she gained a few pounds instead!

My girlfriend did what is probably the best option. She managed to apply for a ground job within the company and spent the next nine months handling M.C. submissions and other utterly boring stuff - just the job for an expectant mother to squeeze in some idle baby talk with the colleagues.

4.   **Your book covers a lot about stewardesses, how about the unsung stewards - I have seen them do all the physical work and seemingly bullied by some stewardesses. Should I still consider joining as a steward?**

Contrary to your fears, the boys in our airline have it great! The cabin crew family have no problems with gender. As for the physically-demanding galley work, what better way for the boys to flex their muscles apart from the rare wrestling down of unruly passengers? The stewards are somewhat like the men behind the successful women, without which the show cannot go on. All play their part in providing a seamless service to the passengers. And if that isn't convincing enough, the prospects of eye-candy at work should entice.

5.   **How is the foreign crew scheduled? Do they only serve on flights to and from their countries of origin?**

The airline employs mainland-Chinese, Japanese, Korean and Indian nationals. It makes economic sense to deploy them according to specific routes that require their language expertise. Yes, they are our flying expats. Many have been with us for a long stretch, blending into the culture of their foster country. Thus, don't be surprised to hear a Japanese spout familiar local phrases with ease or a Korean stewardess lauding her favourite prata joint.

6. **I am currently studying for my degree. Like you, I'm not cut out for an academic life. Should I just quit and join the airline? What are my career options should I quit flying later?**

Hell no! If presented an opportunity to live my life again, I would not have quit university. I'll get my degree first then join the airline. Obviously, I say that with the benefit of hindsight. But take my advice - accumulate a wealth of knowledge from your books first before you consider riches of other forms. That is the best accessory you could ever give your head.

Many colleagues took to studying part-time while flying and believe me, it isn't easy to juggle both well. That said, most overcame the odds and joined the growing numbers of graduates among us, many sleepless nights and whiten hairs later. The airline even has a bi-annual scholarship scheme to encourage worthy employees to further their tertiary education, on top of sponsored language courses. Kudos to that!

There are career opportunities abound once you decide to archive those flight manuals for good. Many ex-colleagues who ventured into the insurance, automobile, hotel and real estate industry have carved a name for themselves through sheer hard work, strong customer and people management skills coupled with confidence developed from their exposure to impeccable service standards in the airline. Employers rate us high on the efficiency and efficacy scale. In fact, many have been poached by business leaders while travelling as passengers – they are able to spot a good catch when served by one. Among us are budding entrepreneurs with keen observation skills and an equally gung-ho spirit who went on to launch their own successful businesses. Fish & Co and Bioskin are sterling examples.

So, there certainly is life after flying.

7. **I am just 2 cm short of the required height and I take a while to warm up to strangers, but I am still keen to be a stewardess as I love to travel. Will I still be able to make the cut?**

Two centimeters short? This is a perennial question. Contrary to popular belief, this is not an aesthetic requirement, rather a service requirement - instead of helping the passengers to stow their bags, a height–challenged attendant may not be able to reach the compartment doors in the first place. I know of a stewardess wannabe who missed the mark by just one centimeter. She was given the red card despite doing a major stretch against the measuring tape. Having said that, I don't mean to be a wet blanket. I can only advise based on what I have seen. Don't take my word for it. Give it your best shot, by all means. Perhaps the selection panel may spot other strengths.

To tell the truth, I am not too at home with strangers myself. The crux of the matter is how well you can overcome this.

8. **When you say that a particular choice of main course is no longer available, do you really have none left? Or if I threw enough of a tantrum, one will mysteriously find its way to me?**

Now, what good does it do to lie about the availability of a dish? After all, it's just a meal.

In fact, the crew is allocated an equal ratio of meal choices which is meant for their own consumption after service. A tantrum from you actually translates to one less meal for us. So now you get it? We don't make up stories just so we could land with mountains of untouched casseroles. Each dish has been prepared with TLC from the mammoth kitchen, so sit back, relax and enjoy whatever that's left.

9. **Why must you kneel or lower yourself to talk to us?**

To tell you the truth, the reason for encouraging attendants to kneel next to the comfortably seated passengers is so that the latter need not arch their necks at an awkward angle while interacting with us. It is by no means a sign of subservience, but yet another gesture geared towards excellent customer service. While the aspect of eye-level communication is met, (not really though, now that we are looking up at them) the comfort of the crew is not.

Male passengers in a talkative mood keep us in the daunting position for too long, often leaving us numb. Those hoping to get lucky with a view of the valley are thwarted by a shield in the form of a serving tray.

10. **Can we keep the cutlery, blanket or pillow as a souvenir?**

I wonder why certain passengers would want to have aircraft memorabilia that had gone through zillions of human contact.

Still, if you insist, please don't make us play accomplice, or worse still, witness to your intended crimes. See no evil, hear no evil. That said, please leave that TV monitor alone.

11.   Where exactly is this crew bunk on the plane?

Ah… so you want to ask the secret agent to divulge classified information? Can't do. The crew bunk on other airlines has had its fair share of stowaways in the past, so I can't betray the whereabouts of this mysterious lair of the cabin crew. All I can say is that we do get our beauty rest in a horizontal position for a few hours, depending on flight duration. You really didn't expect us to stay fresh as an orchid after twelve waking hours in the metal capsule, did you?

And yes, double-decked bunks best describe our meager beds. Thin mattresses, tiny pillows with nary a substance and scratchy blankets, all packed into a space-challenged secret location. Bolsters? Don't even think about it.

12.   One of my guy friends complains that his stewardess girlfriend pesters him for a new branded handbag every other month. Friends tried to set me up on a date with a stewardess, but stories of materialistic stewardesses deterred me. Do I take heed and beat a hasty retreat? Or take my chances on a search for a low-maintenance stewardess?

As the Hokkien saying goes - want fresh, want cheap, want a pair of big tits. Personally, other than an angelic face, a gravity-defying tight bod that could breathe through the pores of the uniform and a service-oriented personality which allows her to smile while cursing silently, a stewardess girlfriend is no different from others. All women could do with a little pampering and wooing. No doubt about that. Apply the same techniques as you would with the other lasses. All you need is a little imagination and loads of sincerity. If she's meant to be yours, the piggy bank has the right to remain intact. At least, that's what J Lo said : "Love Don't Cost A Thing!"

13. Which hotels do you stay in? I might plan to stay in the same ones during my business trips to stake out the pretty ones ;)

Piece of advice. The stewardess who had you totally besotted onboard may not be the real McCoy. Minus the false eyelashes, face paint and carefully styled hairdo. Throw in pale complexion, panda eye rings, morning breath, tousled hair (ala Einstein) and an oversized super comfy tee . Still game to stake us out?

14. What is the funniest incident onboard?

Nothing beats this classic joke among the crew, passed down through the generations. And believe me, no one is going to forget this in a while. A stewardess was serving meatballs to a premium class male passenger. Being the ever considerate host, she decided to ask if he preferred the accompanying sauce over the meatballs or on the side. Alas, sometimes good intentions can come out sounding very wrong, as the stewardess unwittingly said in a voice loud enough to be heard across three rows.

"Mr. So-and-so, would you like sauce on your BALLS?"

AFTERWORD

The morning before He left for work, I was an inconsolable wreck. I couldn't write anymore. The writer's block had attacked its latest victim with gusto. After months of furious scribbling and painstaking finger-typing on my pink VAIO, my table was strewn with crushed up notes, each bearing angry slashes of bold ink. Disaster struck thrice when entire chapters were inadvertently wiped out. Each time the panic attack came and dragged my senses southwards. The pain was real. Losing words that I had typed and retyped during endless hot afternoons with nary a pee-break was frustrating to say the least. Was it worth the struggle to continue?

"Maybe I'm not cut out to be a writer!" I screamed.

He looked me straight in the eye and quoted from Eleanor Roosevelt, "What is to give light must endure the burning." I stared silently as He went through my work late into the night. Word by word. This is good stuff, He declared. Don't let anyone tell you otherwise. That jolted me out of self-doubt.

I wonder how He could consider himself to be "only fifty percent of the man he wants to be." That coming from HIM, a man who has accomplished more in life than anyone I know. If there's anyone who makes the most out of twenty-four hours, it's HIM. Yet, the man neither brags nor throws highlights on his achievements. Here I am, seeking the nearest exit when tracks get derailed.

Motivated and somewhat ashamed by the earlier outburst, I trudged on this literary journey.

Plagued by blood-shot eyes, double eye-bags and splitting headaches, night after night, we pored over tens of thousands of words and explored ways of voicing my thoughts.

Looking at the end product of our efforts, I know that the pain was worth every bit. In the process, it had dealt me some invaluable lessons in life as well. I realised that not only had I succeeded in telling my side of the story, but also that of thousands of past, present and future cabin crews.

For the burning I had endured, I hope my book will now shed light.

A woman is like a tea bag - you never know how strong she is until she gets in hot water.

Eleanor Roosevelt

Acknowledgements

Writing this book was not a piece of cake. It would not have broken out of its baking mould had the following not chipped in with essential ingredients, one way or another. Perfect it may not be, just as one man's meat could be another man's poison. But we made it from scratch and proudly served it up. Isn't that part of the fun?

My dear **Dad**, I know my little project took you away from many karaoke afternoons. For the times when you were tired out on the garden couch with the draft still clutched in your hand, I want to say a big sorry and loud thank you! But expect more to come when the Chinese edition goes through your final edit, all 56,000 words of it!

Having you both read through my unpolished draft on MRT rides and late into the night, makes me guilty as much as I am appreciative. Looking at the highlights and red ink circling my atrocious grammatical errors, I felt like I was back in school! So a big thank you, **Celeste and Andy**!

Mum played accomplice some thirteen years ago. She convinced the man who listens to no one but her. And of course, without whom, I would not have the girl-next-door looks to thank for.

The ever anal third-eye, thanks for highlighting the many blind spots and for cracking me up at two in the morning, **Bro**. That made the editing process actually seems fun! But I promise not to laugh into your ears again.

Goh, my good buddy from secondary school, was her usual candid self when she dissected my draft in between busy consultations with her patients. Thanks woman. I needed that.

A hug for the lovedoves, **Marie** and **Gary** for boosting my confidence. You did not give me a flat 'no' when I pushed the manuscript into your hands. **Esther** has eyes of a hawk, swooping down on silly mistakes that slipped me by!

Celestine got down to analyzing all the details after the initial shock at my little 'project'and she came up with, "woman, you better get an editor!" **Alicia** was a darling to comb for glaring flaws.

JT Koh, who gave this novice his frank feedback, without which this book would have taken another form. Thanks for your invaluable cents, JT.

Thank you **Effendy** and **Kamal** of Bob Associates Design Consultants, for taking on this project. Without your beautiful book designs and layout, this book would have been naked.

Special thanks to the three who contributed their expertise generously: **Johnson** of MarketAsia Distributors, **Janice** of ST Commercial Print and **Nanz Chong-Komo**, who wrote me a wonderful piece of foreword despite her busy schedule.

How can I forget my airline, the one that gave me wings to fly in the first place? After a good many years with you and my crew friends, I can safely declare that we are the best and shall remain so.

I am fortunate to have the company of my three darling doggies-sweet **Ah Mei Mei,** doormat **Maggie Sue** and eccentric **Coco Bongo**. Picking after you three gave me a much needed respite from eye-balling my laptop, though I must admit that writing this book had taken our play-time away. To make matters worse, the recent addition of two stray cats - **Pepper** and **Kitty**; three terrapins - **Eeny, Meeny** and **Moe** to the mini zoo, still leaves **Maggie** seriously un-amused.

My **Xiao Baobei,** I believe you came into my life for a reason. Every now and then, I would flash my uniform out just so that you would be reminded that Mummy once flew the skies and that you were the reason why I willingly bade farewell to a life I loved.

A special thank you to **Adrian** – my mentor, friend and partner all rolled into one. You are the driving force behind our first collaboration. Had you not pushed hard enough, (in fact, I think the push turned to shove!) this book would not have taken flight.

ABOUT THE AUTHOR

The younger of two siblings, the author was born into this world a 'tigress'- in accordance with the Chinese Zodiac; her afternoon birth explains the mild temper. Cursed with a fair complexion that darkens in seconds, she avoids the sun like a vampire. Blessed with a love for all things small and/or furry, she grew up surrounded by a mini zoo of bunnies, doves, quails, hamsters, terrapins, chicks, ducklings and dogs.

A former Miss Intercontinental Singapore and Miss Chinatown runner-up, she modeled part-time while in junior college to earn extra pocket money, and it certainly paid better than giving tuition. It was not all glitz and glamour, she concluded; the bitchiness of this tough industry left her wary.

Her current job description matches that of a care taker and poo-picker - that of her three darling doggies, two stray cats, three terrapins and two Japanese Bantam chickens. The 6.30 am wake-up crows drive her mad though.

She is now mother of a hyper-active five year old boy, true to his zodiac year of the monkey - he tests her tolerance level to the limits. Her years of service in dealing with similar traits found in adults have put her in good stead. She loves him to bits.

In her spare time, she dabbles in beaded jewelry - a craft she learnt from a dear passenger en route a horrendously draggy flight to New York. She is addicted to humour; her favourite books are those by Neil Humphrey.

A self-confessed food junkie, she delights in trying to rid the fridge of chocolates in order to make space for home-baked Oreo cheesecakes - one huge chomp at a time!

Despite braving the cold, both bro and I managed weak smiles. The proverbial ugly duckling, after sifting through tons of photos from my younger days, this is the only one I dare to publish.

Truly happy Chew family – Gorgeous Mum, chubby Bro and Super Dad. The description still fits now.

St. Nicks – Growing up in an all-girl environment where I dealt with infatuations, girl cliques who had a bone to pick with me and trying hard to fit in amid it all.

The 'coming of age' years at Anderson JC – When boys started to pay attention and I was crowned prom queen.

A novice at make-up during cabin crew training – Looking too mature for comfort when the face paint strikes.

The wig that did the trick until the itch kicked in. Still, it was the closest I ever got to thick, lustrous hair.

Xiao Gua, rescued off the lonely streets of Taipei. Looking handsome after a bath, lots of blow-drying and many cuddles later.

The 'tigress' and her lion cub at Kruger Park, Johannesburg. I fed this same cub with a bottle of milk; it was a maternal experience.

My favourite spot in London – A tranquil haven in Hyde Park. In summer, feeding the dray of squirrels beats retail therapy any day.

Bonjour from Paris, an afternoon picnic under the Eiffel is a must.

Up close and personal with the
magnificent Sphinx and ancient
pyramids on my second solo trip.
Awesome!

I made it a point to take photos with dogs from all over the world. This handsome devil of an Alaskan Malamute was found in Brisbane.

Cats rule in this little island off the Acropolis of Athens. See if you can spot the canine among the felines.

On top of a little hill in Athens.

VISIT MY OFFICIAL WEBSITE
www.milehiclub.sg

Check out my personal blog and discussion forum where I continue to thrill with the spills, along with my cabin crew friends who love to share their side of the story. Send me your questions and I'll endeavour to answer as many as I can.

Have a burning tale to tell? Be it travelers' woes, travel tips or a new-found food joint you're dying to announce - share them online and the best entries will win an autographed copy of *The Mile Hi! Club*.

If you are or were a member of the cabin crew, we would like to hear from you too. Share with us your experiences, stories and tips on the best places to shop, eat and see all over the world.

Join The Mile Hi! Club now!

We Want You!

Join the PepperConn Online Talent Team (POTT)

Calling all bloggers, writers, editors, content moderators, video producers and designers, earn extra income and increase your profile by joining our online talent team.

PepperConn LLP is a pioneer in Social Media Solutions for enterprises. We create and manage social media projects, campaigns and platforms for SMEs, government agencies and corporations. Projects could be marketing campaigns, publicity and brand awareness campaigns, community creation and online events.

If you are passionately blogging about a hobby, reviewing games and gadgets, writing about the latest fashion trends and shopping tips, where the favourite food haunts are, the latest clubs, your online business or just life in general – tell us about it and join our database of talents. Chances are, somewhere down the road, we will have a project or client that requires your passion and content creation skill sets. What better way to earn a pretty penny from all that blogging!

Depending on the project requirements, we will need part-timers who can commit to a couple of hours a day or a few days a week. You could be a part of a bigger team or an individual contributor, so students will be perfect for such requirements.

We also seek freelance full time professionals who are keen to work on a project basis.

Top talents will be proactively managed and marketed by our talent management unit where we aim to make you the next top online talent. Who knows… you could be the next big thing online. Join us now and be a part of this pioneering online talent team.

Go to **www.pepperconn.com** for more details.

About Us

PepperConn LLP :
Social Media Solutions for Enterprises

THE MILE HI! CLUB : Memoirs of a Stewardess is PepperConn's first foray into self-publishing. As much as we are immensely proud of the product (book), it is only but a means to an end. That end is a proof of concept of PepperConn's enterprise-class social media solutions and what better way to demonstrate that passion and belief than to apply it to our very own product.

PepperConn LLP is a pioneer in **integrated social media solutions** for SMEs, government agencies and corporations. Effective online strategies and deployment goes beyond online advertising, blogs and product/brand ambassador programs - we **create and sustain unique programs** to increase your traffic, community, customer engagement and sales metrics. Where available, the overall solution should be integrated with traditional media platforms.

PepperConn's differentiator is the in-depth knowledge and experience in **traditional media/content management on new media platforms and channels**. We achieve this with **minimal development work and cost** - meaning that by and large, we leverage off platforms that already exist and are free. Coupled with our own unique in-house modules, we enhance and customize our solutions to meet your goals. As much as new and emerging technology is sexy, again, it is but a means to an end.

We create or convert websites, communities and platforms into SOCIAL MEDIA ASSETS.

At the end of it all, we believe that success measurements of any project, campaign or platform is not just qualitative, but quantitative key performance indicators (KPIs) that we will work together to achieve. Our rates are tiered according to the results.

For more information, visit our website : **www.pepperconn.com** or email me at **adrian@pepperconn.com**

Adrian Teo
Founder and CEO
PepperConn LLP